Luis Valdez—Early Works:
Actos, Bernabé and
Pensamiento Serpentino

Arte Publico Press
Houston
Texas

This Arte Público Press edition of *Actos, Pensamiento Serpentino* and *Bernabé* is made possible through a grant from the Ford Foundation.

Recovering the past, creating the future

Arte Público Press
University of Houston
4902 Gulf Fwy, Bldg 19, Rm 100
Houston, Texas 77204-2004

Luis Valdez—Early Works: Actos, Bernabé and Pensamiento Serpentino / Luis Valdez and El Teatro Campesino.
    p.   cm.
  ISBN 978-155885-003-3
    1. Valdez, Luis. Pensamiento serpentino. 1990. II. Teatro Campesino (Organization) III Title: Actos.
PS3572.A387A6   1990
812'.54—dc20   89-35438
                                                                      CIP

12 13 14 15 16 17 18   14 13 12 11 10 9 8

Contents

Preliminary Note on this Edition

The Archives of El Teatro Campesino and The Luis Valdez Collection

In 1985 El Teatro Campesino and Luis Valdez entered into a long term arrangement with the library of the University of California at Santa Barbara, calling for the establishment of two special archival collections on the work of our internationally renowned theatre company and its noted founder, artistic director and resident playwright.

The Archival Project is now an established on-going process, that has already seen the first phase of a massive task of cataloging and duplicating 25 years worth of archival material from El Teatro Campesino, including scripts, published books, dissertations, theses, published reviews, articles and interviews, edited and unedited film and video, photographs, photo negatives, slides, audio recording, historical masks, costumes, props, lighting plots, costume renderings, set and prop designs, posters, press files, organizational papers, and the private papers of Luis Valdez.

Our collection housed at the Colección Tloque Nahuaque of the Library of UCSB and at The Archives of El Teatro Campesino at our Playhouse in San Juan Bautista will provide for continued preservation and ultimately for increased availability for legitimate scholarly research. The publication of this anthology, "Luis Valdez-Early Works: Actos, Bernabé and Pensamiento Serpentino" is within the spirit and objectives of the Archival Project in disseminating our works.

Luis Valdez is recognized as creating a distinct theatrical tradition and, as one writer put it, "...the only living creator of a generic form of theatre." It is our hope that our Archival Project will encourage further interest and analysis of greater scope and depth of our unique history and of our artistic production. We intend to continue to create and evolve the 'work' and to publish and disseminate those works. In fact, we intend to someday write and publish a definitive history of our 25 years.

We hope you enjoy this new installment of some of the early works of Luis Valdez!

Andrés Valenzuela Gutiérrez
Archives Curator & Press Director

Introduction

As part of its 25th Anniversary Celebration, El Teatro Campesino and Founder/Artistic Director Luis Valdez are proud to offer this collection of work which chronicles significant stages of the group's evolution. El teatro Campesino is about evolution. The group has experienced several transformations since its inception on the strike lines of the Delano Grape Strike in 1965 all by design. El Teatro Campesino is a mirror to the dynamism of life which is in constant flux or, according to Valdez, continuously "shedding its dead skin" like the god Quetzalcoatl. Once a new goal or plateau has been attained the process towards the next objective immediately begins.

El Teatro under the guidance of Valdez has always been close to the pulse of life (and death simultaneously). As Maestro Valdez states in his *Notes on Chicano Theatre*, ". . . if La Raza won't go to the teatro then the teatro must go to La Raza." El Teatro was born to express the verisimilitude of the striking campesinos' reality. Contrary to popular belief, the birth of the acto genre was not necessarily a Chicano version of simplistic slapstick agit-prop. Although the acto's initial objective was to propagandize the issues of the strike, its structure was designed to accommodate a healthy mixture of minimalism and humor, combined with a large dose of *corazón*. This formula successfully served as a catalyst to propel the ideas and emotions of the acto through the physical presence of the players in performance. The immediate result of these elements fused together in a meeting hall or on a flat-bed truck was a sense of campesino reality campesino truth. This subjective, elusive quality cut through any superfluous rhetoric or production quality concerns because it was raw and immediate. It was unavoidable, it was there. And it was produced, acted, directed, designed and improvised by the campesinos themselves.

So, did Valdez, fresh from a visit to Castro's Cuba and a brief stint with the San Francisco Mime Troupe, have a pre-determined blue print calculating the successful conception of a theatre movement tucked under his arm when he first arrived in Delano? A blueprint, no. But the man had ideas. Several ideas about the nature of existence, about the complexity of simplicity, about life and death, and about the physical being, *La Tierra* and the universe. Valdez had only the richness and the beauty of his culture to work with. This combined with his ideas, some hand-painted signs and a few crude props ignited into a performance genre that successfully captured and conveyed a social message encoded with beauty, truth, rascuachismo, humor and universality. He used what he thought would work, and he was correct. This then was the birth of El Teatro Campesino and its initial theatrical format, the *acto*.

Also included in this volume is *Pensamiento Serpentino*, a poetic essay that captures the seeds of Valdez's working aesthetics and world view. The core tenet of the document is "...tú eres mi otro yo (...you are my other self). If I love and respect you / I love and respect myself." The dualistic connotation of this idea is present throughout El Teatro Campesino's and Valdez's work, from *Las Dos Caras del Patroncito* to *I Don't Have To Show You No Stinking Badges*, to Theatre of the Sphere workshops conducted by Maestro Valdez. The concept goes beyond simple dualism; it is more dialectical in its working form. It grows through the tension created by a thesis interacting with an antithesis and evolves into a synthesis. Again, constant evolution, Valdez's trademark. Another important feature of *Pensamiento Serpentino* is Valdez's proclamation to turn to our Ancient American ancestors for spiritual and artistic inspiration: "We must become Neo-Mayas/Because Los Mayas really had it together." Valdez cites the highly developed Mayan religion-science complex as an example of Chicano heritage that is not taught in science or history courses. The Ancient American theologic-scientific concept was rich with ritual: pageantry, spectacle, music, chanting, bodies in motion. Valdez asks us to dive into that ancient and rich cultural pool in the development of the aesthetics of a young Chicano Theatre Movement. *Pensamiento Serpentino* was written in 1971.

Tony Curiel
Associate Artistic Director
El Teatro Campesino

Notes on Chicano Theatre

What is Chicano theatre? It is theatre as beautiful, rasquachi, human, cosmic, broad, deep, tragic, comic, as the life of La Raza itself. At its high point Chicano theatre is religion--the huelguistas de Delano praying at the shrine of the Virgen de Guadalupe, located in the rear of an old station wagon parked across the road from DiGiorgio's camp #4; at its low point, it is a cuento or a chiste told somewhere in the recesses of the barrio, puro pedo.

Chicano theatre, then, is first a reaffirmation of LIFE. That is what all theatre is supposed to be, of course; but the limp, superficial, gringo seco productions in the "professional" American theatre (and the college and university drama departments that serve it) are so antiseptic, they are antibiotic (anti-life). The characters and life situations emerging from our little teatros are too real, too full of sudor, sangre and body smells to be boxed in. Audience participation is no cute production trick with us; it is a pre-established, pre-assumed privilege. "¡Que le suenen la campanita!"

Defining Chicano theatre is a little like defining a Chicano car. We can start with a lowriders' cool Merc or a campesino's banged-up Chevi, and describe the various paint jobs, hub caps, dents, taped windows, Virgin on the dashboard, etc. that define the car as particularly Raza. Underneath all the trimmings, however, is an unmistakable product of Detroit, an extension of General Motors. Consider now a theatre that uses the basic form, the vehicle, created by Broadway or Hollywood: that is, the "realistic" play. Actually, this type of play was created in Europe, but where French, German, and Scandinavian playwrights went beyond realism and naturalism long ago, commercial gabacho theatre refuses to let go. It reflects a characteristic "American" hang-up on the material aspect of human existence.

European theatre, by contrast, has been influenced since around 1900 by the unrealistic, formal rituals of Oriental theatre.

What does Oriental and European theatre have to do with teatro Chicano? Nothing, except that we are talking about a theatre that is particularly our own, not another imitation of the gabacho. If we consider our origins, say the theatre of the Mayans or the Aztecs, we are talking about something totally unlike the realistic play and more Chinese or Japanese in spirit. *Kabuki*, as a matter of fact, started long ago as something like our actos and evolved over two centuries into the highly exacting artform it is today; but it still contains pleberías. It evolved from and still belongs to el pueblo japonés.

In Mexico, before the coming of the white man, the greatest examples of total theatre were, of course, the human sacrifices. *El Rabinal Achi*, one of the few surviving pieces of indigenous theatre, describes the sacrifice of a courageous guerrillero, who rather than dying passively on the block is granted the opportunity to fight until he is killed. It is a tragedy, naturally, but it is all the more transcendant because of the guerrillero's identification, through sacrifice, with God. The only "set" such a drama-ritual needed was a stone block; nature took care of the rest.

But since the Conquest, Mexico's theatre, like its society, has had to imitate Europe and, in recent times, the United States. In the same vein, Chicanos in Spanish classes are frequently involved in productions of plays by Lope de Vega, Calderón de la Barca, Tirso de Molina and other classic playwrights. Nothing is wrong with this, but it does obscure the indio fountains of Chicano culture. Is Chicano theatre, in turn, to be nothing but an imitation of gabacho playwrights, with barrio productions of racist works by Eugene O'Neil and Tennessee Williams? Will Broadway produce a Chicano version of "Hello, Dolly" now that it has produced a Black one?

The nature of Chicanismo calls for a revolutionary turn in the arts as well as in society. Chicano theatre must be revolutionary in technique as well as content. It must be popular, subject to no other critics except the pueblo itself; but it must also educate the pueblo toward an appreciation of *social change,* on and off the stage.

It is particularly important for teatro Chicano to draw a distinction between what is theatre and what is reality. A demonstration with a thousand Chicanos, all carrying flags and picket signs, shouting CHICANO POWER! is not the revolution. It is theatre about the revolution. The people must act in *reality*, not on stage (which could be anywhere, even a sidewalk) in order to achieve real change. The Raza gets excited, simón, but unless the demonstration evolves into a street battle (which has not yet happened but it is possible), it is basically a lot of emotion with very little political power, as Chicanos have discovered by demonstrating, picketing and shouting before school boards, police departments and stores to no avail.

Such guerrilla theatre passing as a demonstration has its uses, of course. It is agit-prop theatre, as white radicals used to call it in the '30's: agitation and propaganda. It helps to stimulate and sustain the mass strength of a crowd. Hitler was very effective with this kind of theatre, from the swastika to the Wagneresque stadium at Nuremburg. At the other end of the political spectrum, the Huelga march to Sacramento in 1966 was pure guerrilla theatre. The red and black thunderbird flags of the UFWOC (then NFWA) and the standard of the Virgen de Guadalupe challenged the bleak sterility of Highway 99. Its emotional impact was irrefutable. Its political power was somewhat less. Governor Brown was not at the state capitol, and only one grower, Schenley Industries, signed a contract. Later contracts have been won through a brilliant balance between highly publicized events, which gained public support (marches, César's fast, visits by Reuther, Robert and Ted Kennedy, etc.), and actual hard-ass, door to door, worker to worker organizing. Like Delano, other aspects of the Chicano movement must remember what is teatro and what is reality.

But beyond the mass struggle of La Raza in the fields and

barrios of America, there is an internal struggle in the very corazón of our people. That struggle, too, calls for revolutionary change. Our belief in God, the church, the social role of women, these must be subject to examination and redefinition on some kind of public forum. And that again means teatro. Not a teatro composed of actos or agit-pop, but a teatro of ritual, of music, of beauty and spiritual sensitivity. This type of theatre will require real dedication; it may, indeed, require a couple of generations of Chicanos devoted to the use of the theatre as an instrument in the evolution of our people.

The teatros in existence today reflect the most intimate understanding of everyday events in the barrios from which they have emerged. But if Aztlán is to become a reality, then we as Chicanos must not be reluctant to act nationally. To think in national terms: politically, economically and spiritually. We must destroy the deadly regionalism that keeps us apart. The concept of a national theatre for La Raza is intimately related to our evolving nationalism in Aztlán.

Consider a *Teatro Nacional de Aztlán* that performs with the same skill and prestige as the Ballet Folklórico de México (not for gabachos, however, but for the Raza). Such a teatro could carry the message of La Raza into Latin America, Europe, Japan, Africa—in short, all over the world. It would draw its strength from all the small teatros in the barrios, in terms of people and their plays, songs, designs; and it would give back funds, training and augmented strength of national unity. One season the teatro members would be on tour with the Teatro Nacional; the next season they would be back in the barrio sharing their skills and experience. It would accommodate about 150 altogether, with 20-25 in the National and the rest spread out in various parts of Aztlán, working with the Campesino, the Urbano, the Mestizo, the Piojo, etc.

Above all, the national organization of teatros Chicanos would be self-supporting and independent, meaning no government grants. The corazón de la Raza cannot be revolutionalized on a grant from Uncle Sam. Though many of the teatros, including El Campesino, have been born out of pre-established political groups, thus making them harbingers of that particular group's viewpoint, news and political prejudices, there is yet a need for independence for the following reasons: objectivity, artistic competence, survival. El Teatro Campesino was born in the huelga, but the very huelga would have killed it, if we had not moved sixty miles to the north of Delano. A struggle like the huelga needs every person it can get to serve its immediate goals in order to survive; the teatro, as well as the clinic, service center and newspaper, being less important at the moment of need than the survival of the union, were always losing people to the grape boycott. When it became clear to us that the UFWOC would succeed and continue to grow, we felt it was time for us to move and to begin speaking about things beyond the huelga: Vietnam, the barrio, racial discrimination, etc.

The teatros must never get away from La Raza. Without the palomilla sitting there, laughing, crying and sharing whatever is onstage, the teatros will dry up and die. If the raza will not come to the theatre, then the theatre must go to the raza.

This, in the long run, will determine the shape, style, content, spirit and form of el teatro Chicano. Pachucos, campesinos, low-riders, pintos, chavalonas, familias, cuñados, tíos, primos, Mexican-Americans, all the human essence of the barrio, is starting to appear in the mirror of our theatre. With them come the joys, sufferings, disappointments and aspirations of our gente. We challenge Chicanos to become involved in the art, the life style, the political and religious act of doing teatro.

Luis Valdez
Summer 1970
Fresno, California

The Actos

Nothing represents the work of El Teatro Campesino (and other teatros Chicanos) better than the acto. In a sense, the acto is Chicano theatre, though we are now moving into a new, more mystical dramatic form we have begun to call the mito. The two forms are, in fact, cuates that complement and balance each other as day goes into night, el sol la sombra, la vida la muerte, el pájaro la serpiente. Our rejection of white western European (gabacho) proscenium theatre makes the birth of new Chicano forms necessary, thus, los actos y los mitos; one through the eyes of man, the other through the eyes of God.

The actos were born quite matter of factly in Delano. Nacieron hambrientos de la realidad. Anything and everything that pertained to the daily life, la vida cotidiana, of the huelguistas became food for thought, material for actos. The reality of campesinos on strike had become dramatic, (and theatrical as reflected by newspapers, TV newscasts, films, etc.) and so the actos merely reflected the reality. Huelguistas portrayed huelguistas, drawing their improvised dialogue from real words they exchanged with the esquiroles (scabs) in the fields everyday.

"Hermanos, compañeros, sálganse de esos files."
"Tenemos comida y trabajo para ustedes afuera de la huelga."
"Esquirol, ten verguenza."
"Unidos venceremos."
"¡Sal de ahi barrigón!"

The first huelguista to portray an esquirol in the teatro did it to settle a score with a particularly stubborn scab he had talked with in the fields that day. Satire became a weapon that was soon aimed at known and despised contractors, growers and mayordomos. The effect of those early actos on the huelguistas de

Delano packed into Filipino Hall was immediate, intense and cathartic. The actos rang true to the reality of the huelga.

Looking back at those early, crude, vital, beautiful, power-ful actos of 1965, certain things have now become clear about the dramatic form we were just beginning to develop. There was, of course, no conscious deliberate plan to develop the acto as such. Even the name we gave our small presentations reflects the hard pressing expediency under which we worked from day to day. We could have called them "skits," but we lived and talked in San Joaquin Valley Spanish (with a strong Tejano influence), so we needed a name that made sense to the raza. Cuadros, pasquines, autos, entremeses all seemed too highly intellectualized. We began to call them actos for lack of a better word, lack of time and lack of interest in trying to sound like classical Spanish scholars. De todos modos éramos raza, (quién se iba a fijar?)

The acto, however, developed its own structure through five years of experimentation. It evolved into a short dramatic form now used primarily by los teatros de Aztlán, but utilized to some extent by other non Chicano guerrilla theatre companies through-out the U.S., including the San Francisco Mime Troupe and the Bread and Puppet Theatre. (Considerable creative crossfeeding has occurred on other levels, I might add, between the Mime Troupe, the Bread and Puppet and the Campesino.) Each of these groups may have their own definition of the acto, but the follow-ing are some of the guidelines we have established for ourselves over the years:

> Actos: Inspire the audience to social action. Illuminate
> specific points about social problems. Satirize the
> opposition. Show or hint at a solution. Express
> what people are feeling.

So what's new, right? Plays have been doing that for thou-sands of years. True, except that the major emphasis in the acto is the social vision, as opposed to the individual artist or playwright's vision. Actos are not written; they are created collectively, through improvisation by a group. The reality reflected in an acto is thus a social reality, whether it pertains to campesinos or to batos locos, not psychologically deranged self-projections, but rather, group archetypes. Don Sotaco, Don Coyote, Johnny Pachuco, Juan Raza, Jorge el Chingón, la Chicana, are all group archtypes that have appeared in actos.

The usefulness of the acto extended well beyond the huelga into the Chicano movement, because Chicanos in general want to identify themselves as a group. The teatro archtypes symbolize the desire for unity and group identity through Chicano heroes and heroines. One character can thus represent the entire Raza, and the Chicano audience will gladly respond to his triumphs or defeats. What to a non-Chicano audience may seem like over simplication in an acto, is to the Chicano a true expression of his social state and therefore reality.

Luis Valdez
Fall 1970
Fresno, California

Actos

Luis Valdez
y
El Teatro Campesino

"Los actos son muy interesantes, chistosos, y representan la realidad de la vida del campesino".

—*César Chávez*

Preface

Over the past six years El Teatro has been changing and moving constantly. Moving with and helping along the way the rebirth of Chicano culture that is shaking the American power structure clear down to its calaveras. That pride that belongs to the sons of kings and religious warriors has found its way to the surface past that mentality of colonization and has brought him face to face with the oppressive forces of ignorance. The ignorant *gabacho* who refuses to see him as anything more than a cheap labor supply. The Chicano has a history as ancient and as beautiful as life itself. From this he is able to grasp a new perspective on the world we live in. A perspective and a way of life that does not include the systematic genocide of unwanted races or a technology that is being used only to destroy the very earth that mothered us. The Chicano is crying for reason and sanity to be brought back to the Americas. He is reaching out, exploding into every field of art and technology known to man, some not recognized by the *gabacho*.

El Teatro Campesino is a part of that explosion. It is taking from the old and creating the new. It is putting all the joys, sorrows, history and culture of La Raza on stage to be examined, to be remade, to pass on to others and to show others that there are answers, that things don't have to be this way. And it does it in its own style, its own form, the Acto. This is the most simple way to say come see what you're doing to me, come see what I have to offer. Actos deal with almost every aspect of Chicano life and death. They are created all over the Southwest by Chicanos with an urgency to be heard. Unfortunately few have been written out and published. El Teatro has started to keep record of as many of these as possible, and would now like to share them with you. These are a select few, published in book form so that they can be used everywhere that there is need for them.

Las Dos Caras del Patroncito

1965

First Performance: The Grape Strike, Delano, California on the Picket line

Characters:

Esquirol
Patroncito
Charlie: Armed Guard

In September 1965 six thousand farmworkers went on strike in the grape fields of Delano. During the first months of the ensuing Huelga, the growers tried to intimidate the struggling workers to return to the vineyards. They mounted shotguns in their pickups, prominently displayed in the rear windows of the cab; they hired armed guards; they roared by in their huge caruchas, etc. It seemed that they were trying to destroy the spirit of the strikers with mere materialistic evidence of their power. Too poor to afford la causa, many of the huelguistas left Delano to work in other areas; most of them stayed behind the picket through the winter; and a few returned to the fields to scab, pruning vines. The growers started trucking in more esquiroles from Texas and Mexico.

In response to this situation, especially the phoney "scary" front of the ranchers, we created "Dos Caras." It grew out of an

improvisation in the old pink house behind the huelga office in Delano. It was intended to show the "two faces of the boss."

A FARMWORKER *enters, carrying a pair of pruning shears.*

FARMWORKER: (*To audience.*) ¡Buenos días! This is the ranch of my patroncito, and I come here to prune grape vines. My patrón bring me all the way from Mexico here to California, the land of sun and money! More sun than money. But I better get to jalar now because my patroncito he don't like to see me talking to strangers. (*There is a roar backstage.*) Ay, here he comes in his big car! I better get to work. (*He prunes. The* PATRONCITO *enters, wearing a yellow pig face mask. He is driving an imaginary limousine, making the roaring sound of the motor.*)

PATRONCITO: Good morning, boy!

FARMWORKER: Buenos días, patroncito. (*His hat in his hands.*)

PATRONCITO: You working hard, boy?

FARMWORKER: Oh, sí patrón. Muy hard. (*He starts working furiously.*)

PATRONCITO: Oh, you can work harder than that, boy. (*He works harder.* Harder! (*He works harder.*) Harder! (*He works still harder.*) Harder!

FARMWORKER: Ay, that's too hard, patrón! (*The* PATRONCITO *looks downstage then upstage along the imaginary row of vines, with the farmworker's head alongside his, following his movement.*)

PATRONCITO: How come you cutting all the wires instead of the vines, boy? (*The* FARMWORKER *shrugs helplessly frightened and defenseless.*) Look, lemme show you something. Cut this vine here. (*Points to a vine.*) Now this one. (FARMWORKER *cuts.*) Now this one. (FARMWORKER *cuts.*) Now this one. (*The* FARMWORKER *almost cuts the*

PATRONCITO'*s extended finger.*) Heh!

FARMWORKER: (*Jumps back.*) Ah!

PATRONCITO: Ain't you scared of me, boy? (FARMWOR-KER *nods.*) Huh, boy? (FARMWORKER *nods and makes a grunt signifying yes.*) What, boy? You don't have to be scared of me! I love my Mexicans. You're one of the new ones, huh? Come in from . . .

FARMWORKER: Mexico, señor.

PATRONCITO: Did you like the truck ride, boy? (FARM-WORKER *shakes head indicating no.*) What?!

FARMWORKER: I loved it, señor!

PATRONCITO: Of course, you did. All my Mexicans love to ride in trucks! Just the sight of them barreling down the freeway makes my heart feel good; hands on their sombreros, hair flying in the wind, bouncing along happy as babies. Yes, sirree, I sure love my Mexicans, boy!

FARMWORKER: (*Puts his arm around* PATRONCITO.) Oh, patrón.

PATRONCITO: (*Pushing him away.*) I love 'em about ten feet away from me, boy. Why, there ain't another grower in this whole damn valley that treats you like I do. Some growers got Filipinos; others got Arabs; me, I prefer Mexicans. That's why I come down here to visit you, here in the field. I'm an important man, boy! Bank of America, University of California, Safeway stores, I got a hand in all of 'em. But look, I don't even have my shoes shined.

FARMWORKER: Oh, patrón, I'll shine your shoes! (*He gets down to shine* PATRONCITO'*s shoes.*)

PATRONCITO: Never mind, get back to work. Up, boy, up I say! (*The FARMWORKER keeps trying to shine his shoes.*) Come on, stop it. Stop it! (CHARLIE *"la jura" or "rent-a-fuzz" enters like an ape. He immediately lunges for the* FARMWORKER.) Charlie! Charlie, no! It's okay, boy. This is one of my Mexicans! He was only trying to shine my shoes.

19

CHARLIE: You sure?

PATRONCITO: Of course! Now you go back to the road and watch for union organizers.

CHARLIE: Okay. (CHARLIE *exits like an ape. The* FARMWORKER *is off to one side, trembling with fear.*)

PATRONCITO: (*To* FARMWORKER.) Scared you, huh boy? Well lemme tell you, you don't have to be afraid of him, as long as you're with me, comprende? I got him around to keep an eye on them huelguistas. You ever heard of them, son? Ever heard of huelga? or Cesar Chávez?

FARMWORKER: ¡Oh, sí, patrón!

PATRONCITO: What?

FARMWORKER: ¡Oh, no, señor! ¡Es comunista! Y la huelga es puro pedo. ¡Bola de colorados, arrastrados, huevones! ¡No trabajan porque no quieren!

PATRONCITO: That's right, son. Sic'em! Sic'em, boy!

FARMWORKER: (*Really getting into it.*) ¡Comunistas! ¡Desgraciados!

PATRONCITO: Good boy! (FARMWORKER *falls to his knees hands in front of his chest like a docile dog; his tongue hangs out.* PATRONCITO *pats him on the head.*) Good boy. (*The* PATRONCITO *steps to one side and leans over.* FARMWORKER *kisses his ass.* PATRONCITO *snaps up triumphantly.*) 'At's a baby! You're okay, Pancho.

FARMWORKER: (*Smiling.*) Pedro.

PATRONCITO: Of course you are. Hell, you got it good here!

FARMWORKER: Me?

PATRONCITO: Damn right! You sure as hell aint' got my problems, I'll tell you that. Taxes, insurance, supporting all them bums on welfare. You don't have to worry about none of that. Like housing, don't I let you live in my labor camp, nice, rent-free cabins, air-conditioned?

FARMWORKER: Sí, señor, ayer se cayó la puerta.

PATROCINTO: What was that? English.

FARMWORKER: Yesterday the door fell off, señor. And

there's rats también. Y los escusados, the restrooms, ay, señor, fuchi! (*Holds fingers to his nose.*)

PATRONCITO: Awright! (FARMWORKER *shuts up.*) So you gotta rough it a little. I do that every time I go hunting in the mountains. Why, it's almost like camping out, boy. A free vacation!

FARMWORKER: Vacation?

PATRONCITO: Free!

FARMWORKER: Qué bueno. Thank you, patrón!

PATRONCITO: Don't mention it. So what do you pay for housing, boy?

FARMWORKER: Nothing! (*Pronounced naw-thing.*)

PATRONCITO: Nothing, right! Now what about transportation? Don't I let you ride free in my trucks? To and from the fields?

FARMWORKER: Sí, señor.

PATRONCITO: What do you pay for transportation, boy?

FARMWORKER: Nothing!

PATRONCITO: (*With* FARMWORKER.) Nothing! What about food? What do you eat, boy?

FARMWORKER: Tortillas y frijoles con chile.

PATRONCITO: Beans and tortillas. What's beans and tortillas cost, boy?

FARMWORKER: (*Together with* PATRON.) Nothing!

PATRONCITO: Okay! So what you got to complain about?

FARMWORKER: Nothing!

PATRONCITO: Exactly. You got it good! Now look at me, they say I'm greedy, that I'm rich. Well, let me tell you, boy, I got problems. No free housing for me, Pancho. I gotta pay for what I got. You see that car? How much you think a Lincoln Continental like that costs? Cash! $12,000! Ever write out a check for $12,000, boy?

FARMWORKER: No, señor.

PATRONCITO: Well, lemme tell you, it hurts. It hurts right here! (*Slaps his wallet in his hind pocket.*) And what for? I don't need a car like that. I could throw it away!

FARMWORKER: (*Quickly.*) I'll take it, patrón.

PATRONCITO: Get you greasy hands off it! (*Pause.*) Now, let's take a look at my housing. No free air conditioned mountain cabin for me. No sir! You see that LBJ ranch style house up there, boy? How much you think a house like that costs? Together with the hill, which I built? $350,000!

FARMWORKER: (*Whistles.*) That's a lot of frijoles, patrón!

PATRONCITO: You're telling me! (*Stops, looks toward house.*) Oh yeah, and look at that, boy! You see her coming out of the house, onto the patio by the pool? The blonde with the mink bikini?

FARMWORKER: What bikini?

PATRONCITO: Well, it's small, but it's there. I oughta know, it cost me $5,000! And every weekend she wants to take trips. Trips to L.A., San Francisco, Chicago, New York. That woman hurts. It all costs money! You don't have problems like that, muchacho, that's why you're so lucky. Me, all I got is the woman, the house, the hill, the land. (*Starts to get emotional.*) Those commie bastards say I don't know what hard work is, that I exploit my workers. But look at all them vines, boy! (*Waves an arm toward the audience.*) Who the hell do they think planted all them vines with his own bare hands? Working from sun up to sunset! Shoving vine shoots into the ground! With blood pouring out of his fingernails. Working in the heat, the frost, the fog, the sleet! (FARMWORKER *has been jumping up and down trying to answer him.*)

FARMWORKER: You, patrón, you!

PATRONCITO: (*Matter of factly.*) Naw, my grandfather, he worked his ass off out here. But, I inherited it, and it's all mine!

FARMWORKER: You sure work hard, boss.

PATRONCITO: Juan . . . ?

FARMWORKER: Pedro.

PATRONCITO: I'm going to let you in on a little secret. Sometimes I sit up there in my office and think to myself: I wish I was a Mexican.

FARMWORKER: You?

PATRONCITO: Just one of my own boys. Riding in the trucks, hair flying in the wind, feeling all that freedom, coming out here to the fields, working under the green vines, smoking a cigarette, my hands in the cool soft earth, underneath the blue skies, with white clouds drifting by, looking at the mountains, listening to the birdies sing.

FARMWORKER: (*Entranced.*) I got it good.

PATRONCITO: What you want a union for, boy?

FARMWORKER: I don't want no union, patrón.

PATRONCITO: What you want more money for?

FARMWORKER: I don't want . . . I want more money!

PATRONCITO: Shut up! You want my problems, is that it? After all I explained to you? Listen to me, son, if I had the power, if I had the power . . . wait a minute, I got the power! (*Turns toward* FARMWORKER, *frightening him.*) Boy!

FARMWORKER: I didn't do it, patrón.

PATRONCITO: How would you like to be a rancher for a day?

FARMWORKER: Who me? Oh no, señor. I can't do that.

PATRONCITO: Shut up. Gimme that. (*Takes his hat, shears, sign.*)

FARMWORKER: ¡No, patrón, por favor, señor! ¡Patroncito!

PATRONCITO: (*Takes off his own sign and puts it on farmworker.*) Here!

FARMWORKER: Patron . . . cito. (*He looks down at the "Patrón" sign.*)

PATRONCITO: All right, now take the cigar. (FARMWORKER *takes cigar.*) And the whip. (FARMWORKER *takes whip.*) Now look tough, boy. Act like you're the boss.

FARMWORKER: Sí, señor. (*He cracks the whip and almost hits his foot.*)

PATRONCITO: Come on, boy! Head up, chin out! Look tough,

look mean. (FARMWORKER *looks tough and mean.*) Act like you can walk into the governor's office and tell him off!

FARMWORKER: (*With unexpected force and power.*) Now, look here, Ronnie! (FARMWORKER *scares himself.*)

PATRONCITO: That's good. But it's still not good enough. Let's see. Here take my coat.

FARMWORKER: Oh, no, patrón. I can't.

PATRONCITO: Take it!

FARMWORKER: No, señor.

PATRONCITO: Come on!

FARMWORKER: Chale. (PATRONCITO *backs away from* FARMWORKER. *He takes his coat and holds it out like a bullfighter's cape, assuming the bullfighting position.*)

PATRONCITO: Uh-huh, toro.

FARMWORKER: ¡Ay! (*He turns toward the coat and snags it with an extended arm like a horn.*)

PATRONCITO: Ole! Okay, now let's have a look at you. (FARMWORKER *puts on coat.*) Naw, you're still missing something! You need something!

FARMWORKER: Maybe a new pair of pants?

PATRONCITO: (*A sudden flash.*) Wait a minute! (*He touches his pig mask.*)

FARMWORKER: Oh, no! Patrón, not that! (*He hides his face.* PATRONCITO *removes his mask with a big grunt.* FARMWORKER *looks up cautiously, sees the* PATRON's *real face and cracks up laughing.*) Patrón, you look like me!

PATRONCITO: You mean . . . I . . . look like a Mexican?

FARMWORKER: ¡Sí, señor! (FARMWORKER *turns to put on the mask, and* PATRONCITO *starts picking up* FARMWORKER's *hat, sign, etc. and putting them on.*)

PATRONCITO: I'm going to be one of my own boys. (FARMWORKER, *who has his back to the audience, jerks suddenly as he puts on* PATRONCITO's *mask. He stands tall and turns slowly, now looking very much like a patrón.*)

Suddenly fearful, but playing along.) Oh, that's good! That's . . . great.

FARMWORKER: (*Booming, brusque, patrón-like.*) Shut up and get to work, boy!

PATRONCITO: Heh, now that's more like it!

FARMWORKER: I said get to work! (*He kicks* PATRONCITO.)

PATRONCITO: Heh, why did you do that for?

FARMWORKER: Because I felt like it, boy! You hear me, boy! I like your name, boy! I think I'll call you boy, boy!

PATRONCITO: You sure learn fast, boy.

FARMWORKER: I said shut up!

PATRONCITO: What an act. (*To audience.*) He's good, isn't he?

FARMWORKER: Come here boy.

PATRONCITO: (*His idea of a Mexican.*) Sí, señor, I theeenk.

FARMWORKER: I don't pay you to think, son. I pay you to work. Now look here, see that car? It's mine.

PATRONCITO: My Lincoln Conti . . . oh, you're acting. Sure.

FARMWORKER: And that LBJ ranch style house, with hill? That's mine too.

PATRONCITO: The house too?

FARMWORKER: All mine.

PATRONCITO: (*More and more uneasy.*) What a joker.

FARMWORKER: Oh, wait a minute. Respect, boy! (*He pulls off* PATRONCITO's *farmworker hat.*) Do you see her coming out of my house, onto my patio by my pool? The blond in the bikini? Well, she's mine too!

PATRONCITO: But that's my wife!

FARMWORKER: Tough luck, son. You see this land, all these vines? They're mine.

PATRONCITO: Just a damn minute here. The land, the car, the house, hill, and the cherry on top too? You're crazy! Where am I going to live?

FARMWORKER: I got a nice, air conditioned cabin down in

the labor camp. Free housing, free transportation . . .

PATRONCITO: You're nuts! I can't live in those shacks! They got rats, cockroaches. And those trucks are unsafe. You want me to get killed?

FARMWORKER: Then buy a car.

PATRONCITO: With what? How much you paying me here, anyway?

FARMWORKER: Eighty-five cents an hour.

PATRONCITO: I was paying you a buck twenty five!

FARMWORKER: I got problems, boy! Go on welfare!

PATRONCITO: Oh no, this is too much. You've gone too far, boy. I think you better give me back my things. (*He takes off* FARMWORKER'*s sign and hat, throws down shears and tells the audience.*) You know that damn Cesar Chávez is right? You can't do this work for less than two dollars an hour. No, boy, I think we've played enough. Give me back . . .

FARMWORKER: Get your hands off me, spic!

PATRONCITO: Now stop it, boy!

FARMWORKER: Get away from me, greaseball! (PATRONCITO *tries to grab mask.*) Charlie! Charlie! (CHARLIE *the rent-a-fuzz comes bouncing in.* PATRONCITO *tries to talk to him.*)

PATRONCITO: Now listen, Charlie, I . . .

CHARLIE: (*Pushes him aside.*) Out of my way, Mex! (*He goes over to* FARMWORKER.) Yeah, boss?

PATRONCITO: This union commie bastard is giving me trouble. He's trying to steal my car, my land, my ranch, and he even tried to rape my wife!

CHARLIE: (*Turns around, an infuriated ape.*) You touched a white woman, boy?

PATRONCITO: Charlie, you idiot, it's me! Your boss!

CHARLIE: Shut up!

PATRONCITO: Charlie! It's me!

CHARLIE: I'm gonna whup you good, boy! (*He grabs him.*)

PATRONCITO: (CHARLIE *starts dragging him out.*) Charlie! Stop it! Somebody help me! Where's those damn union organizers? Where's Cesar Chávez? Help! Huelga! Huelgaaaaa! (CHARLIE *drags out the* PATRONCITO. *The* FARMWORKER *takes off the pig mask and turns toward the audience.*)

FARMWORKER: Bueno, so much for the patrón. I got his house, his land, his car. Only I'm not going to keep 'em. He can have them. But I'm taking the cigar. Ay los watcho. (*Exit.*)

Quinta Temporada

1966

First Performance: At Delano, California, during a grape strikers' meeting in Filipino Hall.

Characters:

Campesino	Fall
Don Coyote	Spring
Patrón	The Unions
Winter	The Churches
Summer	La Raza

The farm labor contractor, satirized as the archetypical DON COYOTE *in this acto, is one of the most hated figures in the entire structure of agri-business. He is paid by the growers for having the special skill of rounding up cheap stoop labor in the barrio and delivering it to the fields. The law stipulates that he must provide safe transportation and honest transactions. The sorrowful reality is something else again, ranging from broken down buses that are carbon monoxide death traps to liquor and meager lunches sold at exorbitant prices to the workers. In the field,* DON COYOTE *sits in his air conditioned pickup while the workers suffer the blistering heat or freezing cold of inclement weather. He originally appeared in this acto with the name of real-life contratistas.* DON COYOTE *has earned the unrelent-*

ing hatred of the campesino, but it is ultimately agri-business that condones and protects him. The only solution to the injustices of the farm labor contracting system is the union hiring hall.

In addition to DON COYOTE, *the seasons appear in "Quinta Temporada" as characters. It is necessary to emphasize the effect of summer, fall, winter and spring on the survival of the farmworker. If it rains he is out of a job, and there is no unemployment compesation. Winter or "El Invierno" is thus almost a living, breathing creature to the campesino — a monster, in fact bringing with him humiliation, starvation and disease. If the strikers laughed at winter in this acto, it was because of the real hope offered by the United Farmworkers Organizing Committee, which created a new "fifth" season.*

Enter FARMWORKER *to center stage from S.L. He addresses audience.*

WORKER: Oh, hello — quihúbole! My name is José. What else? And I'm looking for a job. Do you have a job? I can do anything, any kind of field work. You see, I just got in from Texas this morning and I need to send money back to my familia. I can do whatever you want — pick cotton, grapes, melons. (DON COYOTE *enters while* FARMWORKER *is talking. He smiles and comes toward the* FARM-WORKER.)

COYOTE: My friend! My name is Don Coyote and I am a farm labor contractor.

WORKER: En la madre, ¡me rayé! Un contratista. (*The* FARM-WORKER *kisses the contractor's outstretched hand.*)

COYOTE: So you want work, eh? ¿Busca jale? Bueno, véngase pa'ca un momento. (COYOTE *pulls* FARMWORKER *over to S.R.*) Mire, this summer is coming fat, fat! Covered with money! Dollar bills, five dollar bills, ten, twenty, fifty, a hundred dollar bills and all you have to do is . . . (COYOTE *gestures above* FARMWORKER*'s head as if*

holding a wad of money which he now releases.) catch!
(FARMWORKER *pretends to catch money in his hat.
COYOTE moves downstage center.*) Well, what do you
say? Will you work for me?
WORKER: ¡Oh, sí, patroncito! ¡Sí, señor! (*Approaches* COYO-
TE'*s hand out.*)
COYOTE: (*Grasping hand, shaking it.*) A deal is a deal. (*The
PATRONCITO enters on S.R., stomps downstage smoking
a cigar.*)
PATRON: Boy! (DON COYOTE *shoves* FARMWORKER
aside and leaps toward the PATRON, *landing at his feet
and kissing his boots. He rises dusting off the* PATRON.)
Like your patron, eh, boy?
COYOTE: ¡Oh, sí, patrón!
PATRON: Good. You got my summer crew ready, boy?
COYOTE: Sí, señor. (*He motions to* FARMWORKER, *who
hesitates, then comes over to* PATRON. COYOTE *points
to his hat.*) El sombrero, tonto. (*The* FARMWORKER
*removes his hat and stands beside the contractor, both
smiling assininely toward the* PATRON.)
PATRON: Well, I don't much care what he looks like, so long
as he can pick.
COYOTE: Oh, he can pick, patrón! (*The* PATRON *stomps over
to S.L.* COYOTE *elbows the* FARMWORKER *and makes
a gesture, holding his hands widely apart as if describing
how fat summer will be. The* PATRON *at S.L. calls in*
SUMMER.)
PATRON: Summer! Get in here. (SUMMER *is a man dressed
in ordinary workshirt and khaki hat. His shirt and hat,
however, are completely covered with paper money: Tens,
twenties, fifties. He walks in with his arms outstretched, and
continues across the stage at a normal pace.*)
SUMMER: I am the Summer.
WORKER: ¡Ajúa! ¡El jale!
COYOTE: ¡Entrale, mano! (*The* FARMWORKER *attacks the*

SUMMER, *and begins to pick as many dollar bills as his hands can grab. These he stuffs into his back pockets.* DON COYOTE *immediately takes his place behind the* FARMWORKER *and extracts the money from his back pockets and hands it over to the* PATRON, *who has taken his place behind the contractor. This exchange continues until* SUMMER *exits. The* PATRON *then moves to S.R., counting his money.* DON COYOTE *takes the* FARMWORKER *to S.L. Enthusiastically.)* ¡Te aventastes! Didn't I tell you we're going to get rich? Didn't I tell you? (DON COYOTE *breaks off abruptly and goes over to his* PATRON's *side.)* How'd we do, boss?

PATRON: Terrible! We're going to have to ask for a federal subsidy. (*The* FARMWORKER *searches his pockets for money and panics when he can't find a single dollar bill. He spots the* PATRON *with handfuls of money and his panic turns to anger.)*

WORKER: (*To* DON COYOTE.) Hey! Where's my money?

COYOTE: What money?

WORKER: Pos, what? The money I work for all summer.

COYOTE: You know what's wrong with you? You're stupid. You don't know how to save your money. Look at my patrón, how come he always has money?

WORKER: (*Lunging toward* PATRON.) That's my money!

COYOTE: (*Stops him.*) No! I know who has your money. Come here. (*He takes* FARMWORKER *to S.L. again.*) It's . . . (*He points out toward the audience, making a semi-circle from S.L. to S.R., finally stopping at the* PATRON *and pointing at him inadvertantly.)*

PATRON: Hey!

COYOTE: No! Not my patrón! It's Autumn! Autumn has your money.

WORKER: Autumn?

COYOTE: El otoño.

WORKER: Puras papas. I don't believe you.

COYOTE: You don't belive me? (*Faking his sincerity.*) But I swear by my madrecita! (*Pause.*) Still don't belive me, eh? Okay. Do you want to see the truth in action? Well, here's the truth in action! (DON COYOTE *makes a flourish with his arms, and spits on the floor, then stomps vigorously on the spit with his foot. All in a grandoise manner.*)

WORKER: That's it?

COYOTE: La verdad en acción.

WORKER: Well, here goes mine! (FARMWORKER *spits at* DON COYOTE*'s foot, but* COYOTE *pulls it back just in time. He retaliates by spitting toward* FARMWOKER*'s foot.* FARMWORKER *pulls his foot back just in time, as* DON COYOTE *stomps toward it. The* FARMWORKER *now catches* DON COYOTE *off guard by spitting on his face.*)

COYOTE: (*Retreats momentarily, decides to suppress his anger.*) No matter. Look, mano, this autumn is coming FAT! Fatter than last summer. You go to work for me and you'll be rich. You'll have enough money to buy yourself a new car, a Cadillac! Two Cadillacs! You'll be able to go to Acapulco! Guadalajara! You'll be able to send your kids to college! You'll be able to afford a budget! You'll be middle-class! You'll be Anglo! You'll be rich! (*The* FARMWORKER *responds to all of this with paroxysms of joy, squeals of delight.*) So, what do you say? Will you work for me?

WORKER: (*Suddenly deadpan.*) No.

COYOTE: (*Turns away, goes to D.S.C.*) Okay, no me importa! I don't give a damn. Anyway, winter's coming.

WORKER: (*Suddenly fearful.*) Winter?

COYOTE: El invierno!

WORKER: No! (*He rushes toward the contractor, hand outstretched.* DON COYOTE *grabs it quickly, before the* FARMWORKER *can think twice.*)

COYOTE: Lío es lío, yo soy tu tío, grillo.

PATRON: (*At S.R.*) Boy!

COYOTE: (*Whirling around.*) Yes, patrón?

PATRON: (*Stuffing money into his pockets.*) Is my fall crew ready?

COYOTE: Sí, patrón. (DON COYOTE *motions the* FARM-WORKER *over to S.R. The* FARMWORKER *steps forward, hat in hand, with a smile on his face. The* PATRON *moves forward with a grunt and the* FARMWORKER *steps in front of him. The* PATRON *tries to move around him and the* FARMWORKER *moves in front of him again. The* PATRON *finally shoves the* FARMWORKER *aside and goes S.L. The* COYOTE *yells to* FARMWORKER.) A un lado, suato!

PATRON: Fall, come in here, boy. (FALL *comes in. He is a thinner man than* SUMMER. *His work shirt is covered with money, though more sparsely than* SUMMER'*s.*)

COYOTE: ¡Entrale, mano! (*With a shout, the* FARMWORKER *leaps to his work, picking money off the shirt that* FALL *wears. The same* FARMWORKER-DON COYOTE-PA-TRON *arrangement is used until* FALL *is almost off stage at S.R. At this point, the* FARMWORKER *reaches back and accidentally catches* DON COYOTE'*s hand in his back pocket. Spotting this, the* PATRON *rapidly crosses to D.S.L.*)

WORKER: Hey! That's my money! You're stealing my money! Pos, mira, qué hijo de . . . (FARMWORKER *strikes at contractor.* DON COYOTE *knocks him down and kicks him three times. The* PATRON *stands watching all of this, then finally calls out.*)

PATRON: You, boy!

COYOTE: (*In a sweat, fearful of reprimand.*) ¿Sí, patroncito? I didn't mean it, boss. (*Pointing to his foot.*) Mira, rubber soles, patrón. (DON COYOTE *obsequiously slides over to the boss. The* PATRON *is expansive, beaming, pleased.*)

PATRON: I like the way you do that, boy.

33

COYOTE: You do? Oh, I can do it again, patrón. (*He runs over to the* FARMWORKER *and gives him one final kick in the ribs. The* FARMWORKER *groans.*)

PATRON: (*With corporate pride.*) Beautiful! If there's anything we need in our company, boy, it's discipline and control of our workers!

COYOTE: Sí, señor, disciplina, control de los mexicanos!

PATRON: And just to show you our appreciation for what you do for the business, the corporation, I am going to give you a little bonus. (*Above the flat behind* PATRON *and contractor, a hand appears holding a huge bone with big black letters spelling out the word "bonus." The* PATRON *picks this up and hands it to the contractor.*)

COYOTE: (*Overcome with emotion.*) ¡Oh, patrón! ¡Un hueso! (*There is a loud rumbling noise backstage. Snowflakes come tumbling over the flats.* COYOTE *runs to S.R.*) Winter is coming! (*The* FARMWORKER *picks himself up off the floor and cowers at U.S.C.* PATRON *stands S.L., undistrubed by the advent of* WINTER. *With a final rumble* WINTER *leaps into the scene around the corner of the flat at S.L.*)

WINTER: I am Winter and I want money. Money for gas, lights, telephone, rent. (*He spots the contractor and rushes over to him.*) Money! (DON COYOTE *gives him his bonus.* WINTER *bites the bone, finds it distasteful, throws it backstage over the flats. He whirls around toward the* PATRON.)

COYOTE: Money!

PATRON: (*Remaining calm.*) Will you take a check?

WINTER: (*Rushing over to him.*) No, cash!

PATRON: Okay, here! (*Hands him a small wad of bills.*) Well, that's it for me. I'm off to Acapulco 'til next spring. (*Exits S.L.*)

COYOTE: And I'm off to Las Vegas. (*Exits S.R.*)

WORKER: And I'm off to eat frijoles! (WINTER *nabs the* FARMWORKER *as he tries to escape.*)

WINTER: Ha, ha, Winter's got you! I want money. Give me money!

WORKER: I don't have any. I'm just a poor farmworker.

WINTER: Then suffer! (WINTER *drags the* FARMWORKER *D.S.C., kicking and beating him, then dumps snow on him from a small pouch. The* FARMWORKER *shivers helplessly.* SPRING *enters at S.L., singing a happy tune.*)

SPRING: (*Skipping in.*) La, la, la, la, la. (*Stops, sees* WINTER *maltreating* FARMWORKER.) What are you doing here?

WINTER: Mamasota, who are you?

SPRING: I am Spring, la primavera, but your time is past. You have to go!

WINTER: Some other time, baby.

SPRING: Aw, come on now, you've had your turn. You've got to leave. (WINTER *ignores her with a grunt.*) Get the hell out of here!

WINTER: All right, I'm going for now, but I'll be back again next year, campesino. (*Exits S.R.*)

SPRING: (*Crosses to* FARMWORKER *and helps him to get up.*) There, there, you poor, poor farmworker, here, now, get up. You mustn't let this happen to you again. You've got to fight for your rights!

WORKER: You mean I've got rights?

SPRING: Sure!

WORKER: Ahora, sí. I'm going to fight for my rights like Pancho Villa, like Francisco I. Madero, like Emiliano Zapata . . . (SPRING *startles him by touching his shoulder.*) Ta-ta-ta! (*From backstage is heard the cry: Campesino!*)

SPRING: Oh, my time has come . . . (*Crosses in front of* FARM-WORKER.) I must go now. But, remember, fight for your rights! La, la, la, la. (*Exits S.R., singing and skipping.*)

WORKER: She's right! From now on I'm going to fight for my rights, my lefts, and my liberals. (DON COYOTE *enters S.L.*)

COYOTE: Amigo . . .

WORKER: (*Turns, frightened. Runs to S.R. after* SPRING.) Pri . . .

COYOTE: Pri, what?

WORKER: Pri . . . prepare yourself! You robbed me!

COYOTE: No! No, I'm your friend.

WORKER: Ni madre! You're a thief!

COYOTE: No, soy tu amigo. ¡Somos de la misma raza!

WORKER: ¡Simón, eres rata! (*He swings at* DON COYOTE.)

COYOTE: ¡Calma, hombre! ¡Ahí viene mi patrón!

WORKER: Que venga ese cab . . .

PATRON: (*Enters S.L.*) Boy!

COYOTE: (*Running over to him.*) Yes, boss?

PATRON: You got this year's summer crew ready?

COYOTE: (*Hesitating, hat in hand.*) Well, you see, patrón, it's this way . . .

PATRON: Well?

COYOTE: (*With a forced smiled.*) Sure, boss, it's all ready.

PATRON: Good! (*He turns and crosses to corner of flat at S.L., anticipating the entrance of* SUMMER. DON COYOTE *rushes to* FARMWORKER *at S.R.*)

COYOTE: ¡Andale, mano! You got to work. Haven't I always give you work? Don't I always treat you good?

WORKER: ¡No!

COYOTE: Andale, hombre, be a sport! Do it for old times sake!

WORKER: ¡No, te digo! (*He spots* SUMMER *coming in at S.L.*) ¡Estoy en huelga! (*He squats.*)

PATRON: What's going on? Why isn't he working?

COYOTE: He says he's on strike.

PATRON: Strike? But he can't be! Summer's going by! What does he want?

COYOTE: (*To* FARMWORKER.) ¿Qué quieres?

WORKER: Un contrato bien firmadito.

COYOTE: He wants a signed contract!

PATRON: He's crazy! We need some more workers! Find me some more workers! Find me some more workers!

Summer's passing! (*To audience.*) Five hundred workers! I need five hundred workers! (*Meanwhile,* SUMMER *continues to cross the stage and finally exists S.R. The* PATRON *is frantic, hysterical. He ends up following* SUMMER *off stage. There is a silence. The* PATRON *re-enters in shock and disbelief.*) He's gone. Summer's gone. My crop! Ahhhhhhhh! (*He leaps and snorts like an animal.*)

COYOTE: (*Fearfully.*) ¡Patrón! ¡Patrón! (*The* PATRON *is on the floor, kicking and snorting like a wild horse.* DON COYOTE *leaps on his back and rides him like a bronco until the* PATRON *calms down and settles on all fours, snorting and slobbering incoherently.* COYOTE *pats the side of his head like a horse.*) Chihuahua, cada año se pone más animal mi patrón. It's okay, boss. He can't last, because he's getting hungry. (FARMWORKER *doubles over with pangs of hunger.*) And anyway, here comes Autumn! (AUTUMN *crosses the stage and the* FARMWORKER *approaches him with one hand on his stomach and his other arm outstretched.*)

WORKER: Con esto me compro un taco.

COYOTE: (*Slapping his hand down.*) None of that! Put it here first! (*Stretches out his hand.*)

WORKER: No, I can't. I'm on strike!

COYOTE: No work, no eat! Put it here!

WORKER: No, I . . . (*He hesitates. He is almost ready to take the contractor's hand.* SPRING *enters S.L. dressed as a nun representing the churches.*)

CHURCHES: Wait! (*Crosses to* FARMWORKER.) I am the Churches. I bring you food and money. (*She hands him some cash and fruit.*)

PATRON: (*Back to his senses.*) You . . . you lousy contractor! You lost me my summer crop and my fall crop. You're fired! And you, you communist farmworker. (*Points to nun.*) You, too, you Catholic communist! (*A rumbling noise backstage. The* FARMWORKER *is frightened. He tries to run but the nun holds him. The* PATRON *cowers U.S.C.* SUMMER *enters dressed as "unions" and carries a contract and an oversized pencil.*)

UNIONS: (*D.S.C.*) I am the Unions. We're with you, brother! Keep fighting! (*Crosses to* FARMWORKER *and shakes his hand and stands by his side. There is another rumbling noise backstage.* FALL *re-enters dressed as a Mexican revolutionary representing "la raza."*

LA RAZA: La raza está contigo, mano. Sigue luchando. (*He also joins the ranks around the* FARMWORKER. *One final gigantic rumble from backstage. With snow spilling over the flats,* WINTER *enters with a vengeance.*)

WINTER: ¡Llegó el lechero! And my name ain't Granny Goose, baby! Money, give me money! (*He charges toward the* FARMWORKER *and is repulsed by the* CHURCHES, LA RAZA, *and the* UNIONS *who shout "No!"*) That's what I like, spunk! (*He tries again and is repulsed a second time.*) God damn!!! (*He tries one final time, making himself as big and as frightening as possible, but he fails again. He asks them.*) Who has money? (CHURCHES, UNIONS *and* LA RAZA *point at* PATRON *and shout: "he has." With a gleeful shout,* WINTER *assails the* PATRON, *demanding money. The* PATRON *pulls out money from all of his pockets, wads and wads of it, until he runs out.*) More!

PATRON: That's all I have!

WINTER: More!

PATRON: I don't have any more. Except what I have in the bank. (*With a savage look in his eyes,* WINTER *takes a step backward and gets ready to leap at the* PATRON*'s throat. The* PATRON *is transfixed with fear. He is unable to move until* WINTER *grabs him by the throat and drags him D.S.C.*)

PATRON: But I don't have any money.

WINTER: Then freeze to death! (WINTER *kicks and beats the* PATRON *and pours snow all over him. The* PATRON *shivers and looks up toward the* CHURCHES, UNIONS *and* RAZA.)

PATRON: Help me!

UNIONS: (*With* RAZA *and* CHURCHES.) Sign a contract!

WORKER: ¡Firma un contrato!

PATRON: (*After a pause.*) All right! (UNIONS *hand the* FARMWORKER *the contract and the pencil. The* FARM-WOKER *comes forward and hands them to the* PATRON. *In panic,* DON COYOTE *comes around and kneels beside his boss.*)

COYOTE: No, patrón, don't sign! I'll be out of a job. I brought you wetbacks. They're communists. Nooooo! (*The* PATRON *signs the contract and hands it to the* FARM-WORKER *who looks at it in disbelief.*)

WORKER: $2.00 an hour . . . restrooms in the fields . . . vacations with pay . . . GANAMOS!!!! (*The* FARMWORKER'*s supporters give out a cheer and pick him up on their shoulders and carry him out triumphantly. The* PATRON *crawls out on his hands and knees in the opposite direction.* DON COYOTE *tries to sneak out with the crowd, but* WINTER *catches him.*)

WINTER: Ah-hah! Winter's got you!

COYOTE: (*Bluffing.*) Winter? Hah! Winter's already past! (WINTER *slaps his forehead stupidly.* DON COYOTE *laughs and starts to walk out. Then suddenly* WINTER *snaps his fingers as if realizing something.*)

WINTER: The fifth season! I'm the fifth season!

COYOTE: What fifth season? There are only four!

WINTER: (*Tearing off the top layer of the sign hanging from his neck, revealing a new sign underneath.*) ¡La justicia social!

COYOTE: Social justice? Oh, no! (WINTER *kicks* DON COY-OTE *offstage, then turns toward the audience.*)

WINTER: Si alguien pregunta que pasó con ese contratista chueco, díganle que se lo llevó la quinta chin . . . ¡¡¡La quinta temporada!!! (*Exits S.L.*)

Los Vendidos

1967

First Performance: Brown Beret junta, Elysian Park, East Los Angeles.

Characters:

Honest Sancho
Secretary
Farmworker
Pachuco
Revolucionario
Mexican-American

Scene: HONEST SANCHO's Used Mexican Lot and Mexican Curio Shop. Three models are on display in HONEST SANCHO's shop. To the right, there is a REVOLUCIONARIO, complete with sombrero, carrilleras and carabina 30-30. At center, on the floor, there is the FARMWORKER, under a broad straw sombrero. At stage left is the PACHUCO, filero in hand. HONEST SANCHO is moving among his models, dusting them off and preparing for another day of business.

SANCHO: Bueno, bueno, mis monos, vamos a ver a quién vendemos ahora, ¿no? (*To audience.*) ¡Quihubo! I'm Honest Sancho and this is my shop. Antes fui contratista, pero ahora logré tener mi negocito. All I need now is a customer. (*A bell rings offstage.*) Ay, a customer!

SECRETARY: (*Entering.*) Good morning, I'm Miss Jimenez from . . .

SANCHO: Ah, una chicana! Welcome, welcome Señorita Jiménez.

SECRETARY: (*Anglo pronunciation.*) JIM-enez.

SANCHO: ¿Qué?

SECRETARY: My name is Miss JIM-enez. Don't you speak English? What's wrong with you?

SANCHO: Oh, nothing, Señorita JIM-enez. I'm here to help you.

SECRETARY: That's better. As I was starting to say, I'm a secretary from Governor Reagan's office, and we're looking for a Mexican type for the administration.

SANCHO: Well, you come to the right place, lady. This is Honest Sancho's Used Mexican Lot, and we got all types here. Any particular type you want?

SECRETARY: Yes, we were looking for somebody suave . . .

SANCHO: Suave.

SECRETARY: Debonaire.

SANCHO: De buen aire.

SECRETARY: Dark.

SANCHO: Prieto.

SECRETARY: But of course, not too dark.

SANCHO: No muy prieto.

SECRETARY: Perhaps, beige.

SANCHO: Beige, just the tone. Así como cafecito con leche, ¿no?

SECRETARY: One more thing. He must be hard-working.

SANCHO: That could only be one model. Step right over here to the center of the shop, lady. (*They cross to the* FARM-WORKER.) This is our standard farmworker model. As you can see, in the words of our beloved Senator George Murphy, he is "built close to the ground." Also, take special notice of his 4-ply Goodyear huaraches, made from the rain tire. This wide-brimmed sombrero is an extra added feature; keeps off the sun, rain and dust.

SECRETARY: Yes, it does look durable.

SANCHO: And our farmworker model is friendly. Muy amable. Watch. (*Snaps his fingers.*)

FARMWORKER: (*Lifts up head.*) Buenos días, señorita. (*His head drops.*)

SECRETARY: My, he is friendly.

SANCHO: Didn't I tell you? Loves his patrones! But his most attractive feature is that he's hard-working. Let me show you. (*Snaps fingers.* FARMWORKER *stands.*)

FARMWORKER: ¡El jale! (*He begins to work.*)

SANCHO: As you can see he is cutting grapes.

SECRETARY: Oh, I wouldn't know.

SANCHO: He also picks cotton. (*Snaps.* FARMWORKER *begins to pick cotton.*)

SECRETARY: Versatile, isn't he?

SANCHO: He also picks melons. (*Snaps.* FARMWORKER *picks melons.*) That's his slow speed for late in the season. Here's his fast speed. (*Snap.* FARMWORKER *picks faster.*)

SECRETARY: Chihuahua . . . I mean, goodness, he sure is a hardworker.

SANCHO: (*Pulls the* FARMWORKER *to his feet.*) And that isn't the half of it. Do you see these little holes on his arms that appear to be pores? During those hot sluggish days in the field when the vines or the branches get so entangled, it's almost impossible to move, these holes emit a certain grease that allows our model to slip and slide right through the crop with no trouble at all.

SECRETARY: Wonderful. But is he economical?

SANCHO: Economical? Señorita, you are looking at the Volkswagen of Mexicans. Pennies a day is all it takes. One plate of beans and tortillas will keep him going all day. That, and chile. Plenty of chile. Chile jalapeños, chile verde, chile colorado. But, of course, if you do give him chile, (*Snap.* FARMWORKER *turns left face. Snap.* FARMWORKER *bends over.*) then you have to change his oil filter once a week.

SECRETARY: What about storage?

SANCHO: No problem. You know these new farm labor camps our Honorable Governor Reagan has built out by Parlier or Raisin City? They were designed with our model in mind. Five, six, seven, even ten in one of those shacks will give you no trouble at all. You can also put him in old barns, old cars, riverbanks. You can even leave him out in the field over night with no worry!

SECRETARY: Remarkable.

SANCHO: And here's an added feature: every year at the end of the season, this model goes back to Mexico and doesn't return, automatically, until next Spring.

SECRETARY: How about that. But tell me, does he speak English?

SANCHO: Another outstanding feature is that last year this model was programmed to go out on STRIKE! (*Snap.*)

FARMWORKER: ¡Huelga! ¡Huelga! Hermanos, sálganse de esos files. (*Snap. He stops.*)

SECRETARY: No! Oh no, we can't strike in the State Capitol.

SANCHO: Well, he also scabs. (*Snap.*)

FARMWORKER: Me vendo barato, ¿y qué? (*Snap.*)

SECRETARY: That's much better, but you didn't answer my question. Does he speak English?

SANCHO: Bueno . . . no, pero he has other . . .

SECRETARY: No.

SANCHO: Other features.

SECRETARY: No! He just won't do!

SANCHO: Okay, okay, pues. We have other models.

SECRETARY: I hope so. What we need is something a little more sophisticated.

SANCHO: Sophisti-qué?

SECRETARY: An urban model.

SANCHO: Ah, from the city! Step right back. Over here in this corner of the shop is exactly what you're looking for. Introducing our new 1969 JOHNNY PACHUCO model! This is our fast-back model. Streamlined. Built for speed, low-riding, city life. Take a look at some of these features. Mag shoes, dual exhausts, green chartruese paint-job, dark-tint windshield, a little poof on top. Let me just turn him on. (*Snap.* JOHNNY *walks to stage center with a* PACHUCO *bounce.*)

SECRETARY: What was that?

SANCHO: That, señorita, was the Chicano shuffle.

SECRETARY: Okay, what does he do?

SANCHO: Anything and everything necessary for city life. For instance, survival: he knife fights. (*Snaps.* JOHNNY *pulls out a switchblade and swings at* SECRETARY. SECRETARY *screams.*) He dances. (*Snap.*)

JOHNNY: (*Singing.*) "Angel Baby, my Angel Baby . . ." (*Snap.*)

SANCHO: And here's a feature no city model can be without. He gets arrested, but not without resisting, of course. (*Snap.*)

JOHNNY: En la madre, la placa. I didn't do it! I didn't do it! (JOHNNY *turns and stands up against an imaginary wall, legs spread out, arms behind his back.*)

SECRETARY: Oh no, we can't have arrests! We must maintain law and order.

SANCHO: But he's bilingual.

SECRETARY: Bilingual?

SANCHO: Simón que yes. He speaks English! Johnny, give us some English. (*Snap.*)

JOHNNY: (*Comes downstage.*) Fuck-you!

SECRETARY: (*Gasps.*) Oh! I've never been so insulted in my whole life!

SANCHO: Well, he learned it in your school.

SECRETARY: I don't care where he learned it.

SANCHO: But he's economical.

SECRETARY: Economical?

SANCHO: Nickels and dimes. You can keep Johnny running on hamburgers, Taco Bell tacos, Lucky Lager beer, Thunderbird wine, yesca . . .

SECRETARY: Yesca?

SANCHO: Mota.

SECRETARY: Mota?

SANCHO: Leños . . . marijuana. (*Snap.* JOHNNY *inhales on an imaginary joint.*)

SECRETARY: That's against the law!

JOHNNY: (*Big smile, holding his breath.*) Yeah.

SANCHO: He also sniffs glue. (*Snap.* JOHNNY *inhales glue, big smile.*)

JOHNNY: That's too much man, ese.

SECRETARY: No, Mr. Sancho, I don't think this . . .

SANCHO: Wait a minute, he has other qualities I know you'll love. For example, an inferiority complex. (*Snap.*)

JOHNNY: (*To* SANCHO.) You think you're better than me, huh, ese? (*Swings switchblade.*)

SANCHO: He can also be beaten and he bruises. Cut him and he bleeds, kick him and he . . . (*He beats, bruises and kicks* PACHUCO.) Would you like to try it?

SECRETARY: Oh, I couldn't.

SANCHO: Be my guest. He's a great scape goat.

SECRETARY: No really.

SANCHO: Please.

SECRETARY: Well, all right. Just once. (*She kicks* PACHUCO.) Oh, he's so soft.

SANCHO: Wasn't that good? Try again.

SECRETARY: (*Kicks* PACHUCO.) Oh, he's so wonderful! (*She kicks him again.*)

SANCHO: Okay, that's enough, lady. You'll ruin the merchandise. Yes, our Johnny Pachuco model can give you many hours of pleasure. Why, the LAPD just bought 20 of these to train their rookie cops on. And talk about maintenance. Señorita, you are looking at an entirely self-supporting machine. You're never going to find our Johnny Pachuco model on the relief rolls. No, sir, this model knows how to liberate.

SECRETARY: Liberate?

SANCHO: He steals. (*Snap.* JOHNNY *rushes to* SECRETARY *and steals her purse.*)

JOHNNY: ¡Dame esa bolsa, vieja! (*He grabs the purse and runs. Snap by* SANCHO, *he stops.* SECRETARY *runs after* JOHNNY *and grabs purse away from him, kicking him as she goes.*)

SECRETARY: No, no, no! We can't have any more thieves in the State Administration. Put him back.

SANCHO: Okay, we still got other models. Come on, Johnny, we'll sell you to some old lady. (SANCHO *takes* JOHNNY *back to his place.*)

SECRETARY: Mr. Sancho, I don't think you quite understand what we need. What we need is something that will attract the women voters. Something more traditional, more romantic.

SANCHO: Ah, a lover. (*He smiles meaningfully.*) Step right over here, señorita. Introducing our standard Revolucionario and/or Early California Bandit type. As you can see, he is well-built, sturdy, durable. This is the International Harvester of Mexicans.

SECRETARY: What does he do?

SANCHO: You name it, he does it. He rides horses, stays in the mountains, crosses deserts, plains, rivers, leads revolutions, follows revolutions, kills, can be killed, serves as a martyr, hero, movie star. Did I say movie star? Did you ever see *Viva Zapata*? *Viva Villa, Villa Rides, Pancho Villa Returns, Pancho Villa Goes Back, Pancho Villa Meets Abbott and Costello*?

SECRETARY: I've never seen any of those.

SANCHO: Well, he was in all of them. Listen to this. (*Snap.*)

REVOLUCIONARIO: (*Scream.*) ¡Viva Villaaaaa!

SECRETARY: That's awfully loud.

SANCHO: He has a volume control. (*He adjusts volume. Snap.*)

REVOLUCIONARIO: (*Mousey voice.*) Viva Villa.

SECRETARY: That's better.

SANCHO: And even if you didn't see him in the movies, perhaps you saw him on TV. He makes commercials. (*Snap.*)

REVOLUCIONARIO: Is there a Frito Bandito in your house?

SECRETARY: Oh yes, I've seen that one!

SANCHO: Another feature about this one is that he is economical. He runs on raw horsemeat and tequila!

SECRETARY: Isn't that rather savage?

SANCHO: Al contrario, it makes him a lover. (*Snap.*)

REVOLUCIONARIO: (*To* SECRETARY.) Ay, mamasota, cochota, ven pa 'ca! (*He grabs* SECRETARY *and folds her back, Latin-lover style.*)

SANCHO: (*Snap.* REVOLUCIONARIO *goes back upright.*) Now wasn't that nice?

SECRETARY: Well, it was rather nice.

SANCHO: And finally, there is one outstanding feature about this model I know the ladies are going to love: he's a genuine antique! He was made in Mexico in 1910!

SECRETARY: Made in Mexico?

SANCHO: That's right. Once in Tijuana, twice in Guadalajara, three times in Cuernavaca.

SECRETARY: Mr. Sancho, I thought he was an American product.

SANCHO: No, but . . .

SECRETARY: No, I'm sorry. We can't buy anything but American made products. He just won't do.

SANCHO: But he's an antique!

SECRETARY: I don't care. You still don't understand what we

need. It's true we need Mexican models, such as these, but it's more important that he be American.

SANCHO: American?

SECRETARY: That's right, and judging from what you've shown me, I don't think you have what we want. Well, my lunch hour's almost over, I better . . .

SANCHO: Wait a minute! Mexican but American?

SECRETARY: That's correct.

SANCHO: Mexican but . . . (*A sudden flash.*) American! Yeah, I think we've got exactly what you want. He just came in today! Give me a minute. (*He exits. Talks from backstage.*) Here he is in the shop. Let me just get some papers off. There. Introducing our new 1970 Mexican-American! Ta-ra-ra-raaaa! (SANCHO *brings out the* MEXICAN-AMERICAN *model, a clean-shaven middle class type in a business suit, with glasses.*)

SECRETARY: (*Impressed.*) Where have you been hiding this one?

SANCHO: He just came in this morning. Ain't he a beauty? Feast you eyes on him! Sturdy U.S. Steel frame, streamlined, modern. As a matter of fact, he is built exactly like our Anglo models, except that he comes in a variety of darker shades: naugahide, leather or leatherette.

SECRETARY: Naugahide.

SANCHO: Well, we'll just write that down. Yes, señorita, this model represents the apex of American engineering! He is bilingual, college educated, ambitious! Say the word "acculturate" and he accelerates. He is intelligent, well-mannered, clean. Did I say clean? (*Snap.* MEXICAN-AMERICAN *raises his arm.*) Smell.

SECRETARY: (*Smells.*) Old Sobaco, my favorite.

SANCHO: (*Snap.* MEXICAN-AMERICAN *turns toward* SANCHO.) Eric? (*To* SECRETARY.) We call him Eric García. (*To* ERIC.) I want you to meet Miss JIM-enez, Eric.

MEXICAN-AMERICAN: Miss JIM-enez, I am delighted to

make your acquaintance. (*He kisses her hand.*)

SECRETARY: Oh, my, how charming!

SANCHO: Did you feel the suction? He has seven especially engineered suction cups right behind his lips. He's a charmer all right!

SECRETARY: How about boards, does he function on boards?

SANCHO: You name them, he is on them. Parole boards, draft boards, school boards, taco quality control boards, surf boards, two by fours.

SECRETARY: Does he function in politics?

SANCHO: Señorita, you are looking at a political machine. Have you ever heard of the OEO, EOC, COD, WAR ON POVERTY? That's our model! Not only that, he makes political speeches.

SECRETARY: May I hear one?

SANCHO: With pleasure. (*Snap.*) Eric, give us a speech.

MEXICAN-AMERICAN: Mr. Congressman, Mr. Chairman, members of the board, honored guests, ladies and gentlemen. (SANCHO *and* SECRETARY *applaud.*) Please, please. I come before you as a Mexican-American to tell you about the problems of the Mexican. The problems of the Mexican stem from one thing and one thing only: he's stupid. He's uneducated. He needs to stay in school. He needs to be ambitious, foward-looking, harder-working. He needs to think American, American, American, American, American! God bless America! God bless America! God bless America! (*He goes out of control.* SANCHO *snaps frantically and the* MEXICAN-AMERICAN *finally slumps forward, bending at the waist.*)

SECRETARY: Oh my, he's patriotic too!

SANCHO: Sí, señorita, he loves his country. Let me just make a little adjustment here. (*Stands* MEXICAN-AMERICAN *up.*)

SECRETARY: What about upkeep? Is he economical?

SANCHO: Well, no, I won't lie to you. The Mexican-American

costs a little bit more, but you get what you pay for. He's worth every extra cent. You can keep him running on dry Martinis, Langendorf bread . . .

SECRETARY: Apple pie?

SANCHO: Only Mom's. Of course, he's also programmed to eat Mexican food at ceremonial functions, but I must warn you, an overdose of beans will plug up his exhaust.

SECRETARY: Fine! There's just one more question. How much do you want for him?

SANCHO: Well, I tell you what I'm gonna do. Today and today only, because you've been so sweet, I'm gona let you steal this model from me! I'm gonna let you drive him off the lot for the simple price of, let's see, taxes and license included, $15,000.

SECRETARY: Fifteen thousand dollars? For a Mexican!!!!

SANCHO: Mexican? What are you talking about? This is a Mexican-American! We had to melt down two pachucos, a farmworker and three gabachos to make this model! You want quality, but you gotta pay for it! This is no cheap run-about. He's got class!

SECRETARY: Okay, I'll take him.

SANCHO: You will?

SECRETARY: Here's your money.

SANCHO: You mind if I count it?

SECRETARY: Go right ahead.

SANCHO: Well, you'll get your pink slip in the mail. Oh, do you want me to wrap him up for you? We have a box in the back.

SECRETARY: No, thank you. The Governor is having a luncheon this afternoon, and we need a brown face in the crowd. How do I drive him?

SANCHO: Just snap your fingers. He'll do anything you want. (SECRETARY *snaps.* MEXICAN-AMERICAN *steps forward.*)

MEXICAN-AMERICAN: ¡Raza querida, vamos levantando

armas para liberarnos de estos desgraciados gabachos que nos explotan! Vamos . . .

SECRETARY: What did he say?

SANCHO: Something about taking up arms, killing white people, etc.

SECRETARY: But he's not supposed to say that!

SANCHO: Look, lady, don't blame me for bugs from the factory. He's your Mexican-American, you bought him, now drive him off the lot!

SECRETARY: But he's broken!

SANCHO: Try snapping another finger. (SECRETARY *snaps.* MEXICAN-AMERICAN *comes to life again.*)

MEXICAN-AMERICAN: Esta gran humanidad ha dicho basta! ¡Y se ha puesto en marcha! ¡Basta! ¡Basta! ¡Viva la raza! ¡Viva la causa! ¡Viva la huelga! ¡Vivan los brown berets! ¡Vivan los estudiantes! ¡Chicano power! (*The* MEXICAN-AMERICAN *turns toward the* SECRETARY, *who gasps and backs up. He keeps turning toward the* PACHUCO, FARMWORKER *and* REVOLUCIONARIO, *snapping his fingers and turning each of them on, one by one.*)

PACHUCO: (*Snap. To* SECRETARY.) I'm going to get you, baby! ¡Viva la raza!

FARMWORKER: (*Snap. To* SECRETARY.) ¡Viva la huelga! ¡Viva la huelga! ¡Viva la huelga!

REVOLUCIONARIO: (*Snap. To* SECRETARY.) ¡Viva la revolución! (*The three models join together and advance toward the* SECRETARY, *who backs up and runs out of the shop screaming.* SANCHO *is at the other end of the shop holding his money in his hand. All freeze. After a few seconds of silence, the* PACHUCO *moves and stretches, shaking his arms and loosening up. The* FARMWORKER *and* REVOLUCIONARIO *do the same.* SANCHO *stays where he is, frozen to his spot.*)

JOHNNY: Man, that was a long one, ese. (*Others agree with him.*)

FARMWORKER: How did we do?

JOHNYY: Pretty good, look at all that lana, man! (*He goes over to* SANCHO *and removes the money from his hand.* SAN-CHO *stays where he is.*)

REVOLUCIONARIO: En la madre, look at all the money.

JOHNNY: We keep this up, we're going to be rich.

FARMWORKER: They think we're machines.

REVOLUCIONARIO: Burros.

JOHNNY: Puppets.

MEXICAN-AMERICAN: The only thing I don't like is how come I always get to play the goddamn Mexican-American?

JOHNNY: That's what you get for finishing high school.

FARMWORKER: How about our wages, ese?

JOHNNY: Here it comes right now. $3,000 for you, $3,000 for you, $3,000 for you and $3,000 for me. The rest we put back into the business.

MEXICAN-AMERICAN: Too much, man. Heh, where you vatos going tonight?

FARMWORKER: I'm going over to Concha's. There's a party.

JOHNNY: Wait a minute, vatos. What about our salesman? I think he needs an oil job.

REVOLUCIONARIO: Leave him to me. (*The* PACHUCO, FARMWORKER *and* MEXICAN-AMERICAN *exit, talking loudly about their plans for the night. The* REVOLUCIONARIO *goes over to* SANCHO, *removes his derby hat and cigar, lifts him up and throws him over his shoulder.* SANCHO *hangs loose, lifeless. To audience.*) He's the best model we got! ¡Ajúa! (*Exit.*)

La Conquista de Mexico
(A Puppet Show)

1968

First Performance: At El Centro Campesino Cultural, Del Rey, California.

Characters:

Piedra del Sol
Moctezuma II
Cempoala
Tlaxcala & Son
Cholula
Hernán Cortez
Fray Bartolo
La Malinche
Teomama
Cuauhtemoc

Música indígena. Drums and flutes. In front of a bright red cloth screen is the Aztec calendar stone — la piedra del sol. The sun face at the center of the stone narrates the story.

PIEDRA: In the Aztec year of Ce-Acatl, which was called 1519 by the gabachos and the gachupines, there was a great city in the Valley of Mexico which was called Tenochtitlán. The chief of this great civilization was noble prince and religious warrior called Moctezuma Xocoyotzin el Segundo.

MOCTEZUMA: (*Appears.*) El primero fue el jefe de mi jefito, mi abuelito.

PIEDRA: His warriors had almost conquered the entire world. Many tribes and many cities lived in fear of Moctezuma. Only the Mayas of Yucatán had not been conquered by Tenochtitlán.

MOCTEZUMA: Me faltan los mayas, pero mulas más peores me he echado.

PIEDRA: Cempoala, Tlaxcala and Cholula were among the tribes that paid tribute to Mexico.

MOCTEZUMA: Ahora, indios raros, a pagar la renta se ha dicho.

PIEDRA: All these tribes had all been conquered by the Aztecs, so instead of fighting Moctezuma they fought each other. Se la pasaban agarrados del moco. (*Indios start to fight and* MOCTEZUMA *shuts them up.*)

MOCTEZUMA: ¡Cállense! ¿Que no miran que tengo una migraine headache? Ahora, ¡Cempoala!

CEMPOALA: (*Comes forward.*) ¿Sí, mi rey?

MOCTEZUMA: ¿Qué me traes?

CEMPOALA: Le traigo chocolate, cacahuates y diez botellas de Thunderbird wine.

MOCTEZUMA: Ay, qué bueno, pásale, pásale. (CEMPOALA *backs away.*) ¡Cholula!

CHOLULA: (*Comes forward, bows.*) ¿Sí, mi rey?

MOCTEZUMA: ¿Qué me traes?

CHOLULA: Cobijas, plumas finas y oro, mi rey.

MOCTEZUMA: Y no es Westinghouse electric blanket?

CHOLULA: No, mi rey.

MOCTEZUMA: Bueno, pues, pásale, pásale. (CHOLULA

backs away.) ¡Tlaxcala!

TLAXCALA: (*Comes forward.*) ¿Sí, mi majestad?

MOCTEZUMA: ¿Qué me traes?

TLAXCALA: Chiles y frijoles.

MOCTEZUMA: O, y un esclavo, ¿verdad?

TLAXCALA: No, señor, es m'ijo.

MOCTEZUMA: Bueno, pues, sígale, sígale.

TLAXCALA: ¿Querías más? Pediche. (*Starts to back off.*)

MOCTEZUMA: ¿Que qué?

TLAXCALA: A que soy sanavaviche, señor.

MOCTEZUMA: Ese insulto me lo vas a pagar, y ahora quiero un sacrificio. Y tu hijo será suficiente.

TLAXCALA: Pero es m'ijo, señor.

MOCTEZUMA: No le hace.

TLAXCALA: ¡Sí, le hace!

MOCTEZUMA: Si no das la vida de tu hijo, morirán más de tu gente. (*Calls.*) ¡Teomama! ¡Teomama!

TEOMAMA: (*Entering.*) ¿Sí, mi rey?

MOCTEZUMA: Mira, aquí tenemos un sacrificio para nuestros dioses. Go do your duty, man.

TEOMAMA: Simón. Vente pa'ca m'ijito. (*Grabs* TLAXCALA*'s son.*)

SON: Papi, papi, ¿qué me están haciendo? (TEOMAMA *bends him backward.*)

MOCTEZUMA: ¡Alabado sea el nombre de huichilobos! (TEOMAMA *sacrifices* TLAXCALA*'s son.*)

SON: Ouchy, ouchy, ouchy. (*He goes limp.*)

MOCTEZUMA: Ahora, Teomama, pon atención. Llévate este cuerpo y hazme unas enchiladas, ¿me entiendes?

TEOMAMA: ¿Con guacamole mi rey?

MOCTEZUMA: Correcto. (TEOMAMA *exits with* SON*'s body.*) Qué corazonzote tenía ese huerco.

TLAXCALA: (*With hate.*) Por eso me lo vas a pagar.

MOCTEZUMA: ¿Que qué?

TLAXCALA: (*Suddenly fearful.*) A que no sé dónde parar ... me.

MOCTEZUMA: ¿Cómo que párate? ¿Todavía están aquí? Indios huevones, mitoteros! ¡Píntense! Pero aquí los quiero el primero del mes con la renta. ¡Lárguense!

PIEDRA: And so Moctezuma was a powerful prince.

MOCTEZUMA: Te estás dando cuenta, ¿eh? ¿Vale?

PIEDRA: But inspite of all his power, there was something that bothered him very much.

MOCTEZUMA: ¡En la madre!

PIEDRA: The year Ce-Acatl was the year in which the great white bearded god — the feathered serpent — Quetzalcóatl was to return to México.

MOCTEZUMA: Y si llega ese pelado, me va agüitar el hueso.

PIEDRA: His priests told him of omens and forebodings that were appearing across the land. (TEOMAMA *enters and goes to* MOCTEZUMA. *They pantomime conversation.*) A great ball of fire crossed the heavens in broad daylight . . .

VOICES: (*Including* TEOMAMA *and* MOCTEZUMA.) ¡Ayyyy!

PIEDRA: The temple of Huitzilopotchli burst into flames by itself . . .

VOICES: Ayyyyyy!

PIEDRA: A strange woman ran through the streets weeping and screaming . . .

VOICES: Ayyyyy!

MOCTEZUMA: ¡Ya córtale! ¿Que no miras que me estás asustando? (TEOMAMA *exits.*)

PIEDRA: All these were the signs that foretold the coming of . . .

MOCTEZUMA: Quetzalcóatl!

PIEDRA: Then one day Moctezuma received word that some white strangers had appeared on the land. (TEOMAMA *re-enters.*)

TEOMAMA: ¡Mi rey, mi rey!

MOCTEZUMA: No grites. No estoy sordo. ¿Qué quieres?

TEOMAMA: ¡Han llegado unos hombres blancos y barbudos del mar! ¡Se me hace que son gabachos!

MOCTEZUMA: ¿Cómo que gabachos? ¡Todavía no los inventan! Vamos al templo.

PIEDRA: The great prince rose and went to the temple of Quetzalcóatl to see if the white god had truly returned to México.

MOCTEZUMA: (*Arms up to the heavens.*) Quetzal! . . . Quetzalcóatl. ¿Estás allá arriba?

PIEDRA: (*Imitating God.*) ¡¡¡¡Chale!!!!

MOCTEZUMA: ¡Oh! ¡Chihuahua! Ya cuando se estaba poniendo a toda madre, tiene que bajar pa' meter su cucharota.

PIEDRA: ¡¡¡¡Que qué!!!!!

MOCTEZUMA: Ah, no digo nada, alabado sea el nombre de Quetzalcóatl. Oye, Teomama, pon atención. Lleva estas plumas finas y este oro y dáselos a esos gringos y diles que ya no hay. ¡Que se secó la vaca! Oh sí, otro mensaje. (MOCTEZUMA *whispers in his ear.*)

TEOMAMA: Orale, hay te watcho. (*Exits.*)

MOCTEZUMA: ¡Qué dolor de cabeza tengo! Vale más ir al templo de Huichilobos a rezar mis oraciones y a recibir la sagrada mota. (*Turns.*) Sacerdotes, preparen mis leños, porque en estos momentos vamos a dejarnos cae . . . (*He exits.*)

PIEDRA: The white men were not gods, but Spaniards. They came mounted on horrible four-legged beasts. (CORTEZ *comes riding in on a horse.*)

CORTEZ: Woah there, boy, woah.

PIEDRA: The chief of the white men was a bearded coyote named Hernán Cortez.

CORTEZ: You can just call me Hernán.

PIEDRA: With him was another white devil named Pedro de Alvarado.

PETE: (*Galloping in on a horse.*) Woah, there, boy, woah! (*He puts horses away. Salutes* CORTEZ.)

CORTEZ: Well, Pete, did you park the car?

PETE: Yeah, boss.

PIEDRA: And finally there was a pale hairless fat man who served as their chief sorcerer, Fray Bartolo.

BARTOLO: (*Comes in on a donkey.*) Woah, there, Jennie, I said woah.

CORTEZ: Hello, father.

BARTOLO: Hello, my son. (*All huddle together and begin to plan. Then they scatter in three directions.*)

PIEDRA: They came in search of a yellow metal which they considered to be more valuable even than jade or chocolate or even the sacred feathers of the Quetzal. They called this metal El Gold.

CORTEZ: Gold! Who said gold?

BARTOLO: Gold!

PETE: (*Pointing to* PIEDRA.) That man with the funny face said gold.

PIEDRA: The first tribe they met and conquered was Cempoala. (*Drums begin to sound.*)

CORTEZ: What's that?

PETE: Injuns!!

CORTEZ: Well, let's get ready to baptize him.

BARTOLO: Yeah. (CEMPOALA *comes in.*)

CEMPOALA: How!!

BARTOLO: Here's how! (*Beats him over the head with cross.*) I baptize you in the name of the Father, the Son and the Holy Ghost and the Catholic religion. Now Sunday school will start Monday morning at 10: 00 a.m. . . . .

CORTEZ: Hold on, father! That's enough for the Lord's business, and now for the king's!

PETE: (*Beating* CEMPOALA *over the head.*) Where's the gold, you stupid spic? You greaser! (*Slaps him around.*)

CEMPOALA: Ay, ay! Yo no, señores. ¡El gold está con Tlaxcala! ¡Tlaxcala!

PETE: Trascala, Trascala? Where's Trascala?

MALINCHE: (*Appears.*) I know where Tlaxcala's at. (PETE *gives a wolf whistle.*)

PIEDRA: And here is where La Malinche steps into the story.

MALINCHE: Well, it was about time! ¿Me hablaba jefito?

CEMPOALA: Sí, m'ija. Mira, quiero que te lleves a estos gabachos pa' Tlaxcala. Diles que aquí no hay gold ni nada. ¿Me entiendes?

MALINCHE: Sí, jefito. (CEMPOALA *exits.* MALINCHE *crosses to Spaniards.*) Hello boys.

PETE: She speaks our lingo!

CORTEZ: She sure speaks my lingo. Father, let's baptize this poor heathen child.

BARTOLO: Sounds like a good idea. Stand back, my child, you are about to be baptized. I baptize you in the name of the Father, the Son, the Holy Ghost and the Catholic religion. And now for a little holy communion. (*Starts to exit with* MALINCHE.)

CORTEZ: Father, that's the king's business. And I being the official representative of the king, in other words, sock it to me, baby! (*He dissappears with* MALINCHE.)

PETE: (*Sings.*) Don't go under the cactus tree with anyone else but me
Anyone else but me
Anyone else but me
No, no, no
Don't go under the cactus tree . . .

CORTEZ: (*Re-appears alone.*) Come on, gang.

PETE: Yahoo, where's the cactus tree?

BARTOLO: Where do I lay my cross?

PIEDRA: This woman was to become infamous in the history of Mexico. Not only did she turn her back on her own people, she joined the white men and became assimilated, serving as their guide and interpreter and generally assisting in the conquest. She was the first Mexican-American.

MALINCHE: (*Re-appears alone.*) Huy, huy, ¡qué escándalo! Y si me gustan los güeritos, ¿qué? Come in Hernán, mi honito, no les hagas caso. (CORTEZ *and* PETE *reappear.*)

CORTEZ: I like this child.
PETE: Yeah, boss, let's go. (*The three start to exit. Then* TEOMAMA *comes running in.*)
TEOMAMA: ¡Espérale! ¡Espérale! Aquí les traigo un mensaje de mi rey Moctezuma.
PETE: What did he say?
MALINCHE: He says he has a message from his king Moctezuma.
CORTEZ: What is it?
TEOMAMA: Les manda plumas finas y oro para los dioses blancos.
MALINCHE: He brings precious feathers and gold for the white gods.
CORTEZ: Gods! Did you hear that, Pete? He called us gods.
PETE: Well, I'll be goddamned.
TEOMAMA: Y otro mensaje, "Yankee go home!"
CORTEZ: Go home, my Aztec! With all this gold, this is my home! Hey, boy, where is this Mexico?
TEOMAMA: (*Acting stupid.*) Oh, señor, I don't know. She is far away. I think. My name es José Jiménez. (*Exits.*)
MALINCHE: I'll show you the way, Hernán.
CORTEZ: I like that child more and more.
PIEDRA: The next tribe the conquistadores met was Tlaxcala, and there they encountered a strong defense.
TLAXCALA: Simón, ¡los de Tlaxcala son muy machos!
PIEDRA: But the gachupines were not alone. Cempoala had joined them in order to fight his most hated enemy, Tlaxcala.
CEMPOALA: Indio mugroso, ¿quieres pedo?
TLAXCALA: Pos, ponte.
CEMPOALA: ¡Orale! (*They fight.* TLAXCALA *is defeated.*) ¡Te vencimos!
TLAXCALA: Sí, pero con la ayuda de esos dioses blancos.
CEMPOALA: Chale. Si yo solo he peleado. (*They start to fight again.*)
PETE: Hey, cool it. Disperse, disperse.

MALINCHE: Hernán. (*She whispers in his ear.*)

CORTEZ: You're right! Hey, Pete?

PETE: Yeah, boss.

CORTEZ: Get your buns over here.

PETE: I'll be back, you guys, so watch it. (*He goes over to* CORTEZ.) Yeah, boss, what do you want?

CORTEZ: Did you tell those stupid Indians to get along together?

PETE: Yeah.

CORTEZ: Don't you know that there are more of them than there are of us?

PETE: No.

CORTEZ: Do you know what would happen if they got together.

PETE: What?

CORTEZ: It'd be curtains for us.

PETE: Hey, boss, you're pretty smart. I never thought of that.

CORTEZ: Of course. I went to Fresno State College. (*To* MALINCHE.) Honey, ask them where the gold is.

MALINCHE: El señor Cortez quiere saber dónde está el oro.

TLAXCALA: (*Acting stupid.*) ¿Oro?

CEMPOALA: (*Acting stupid.*) ¿Oro?

GLAXCALA: (*Acting stupid.*) Oro who? Oh, el oro! El oro está allá en Cholula.

CORTEZ: Cholula? Where's this Cholula?

MALINCHE: I'll show you, Hernán.

CORTEZ: I like this girl more and more.

PETE: I'm right behind you, boss. (*Looks into the audience.*) Guess what, I think we're gonna get the gold.

CEMPOALA and TLAXCALA: Vamos a Cholula! (*They exit.*)

PIEDRA: The next tribe the conquistadores met was Cholula, and this time they encountered tremendous defense.

CHOLULA: Simón, ¡los de Cholula son matones!

PIEDRA: But the gachupines were not alone. Cempoala and Tlaxcala had joined them in order to fight their most hated enemy, Cholula.

TLAXCALA: ¡Hora, indio roñoso, ¿quieres pedo?

CEMPOALA: ¡Déjamelo a mí! Yo me lo echo.

CHOLULA: Orale, carnales. ¿Qué se traen? ¿Por qué buscan pleito?

TLAXCALA: ¡Porque nos da la gana! ¡Ora, ponte!

CHOLULA: ¿Ya se juntaron con estos gabachos?

CEMPOALA: ¡Sirol! Nos gusta estar en el "winning side."

CHOLULA: ¡Pos, vamos a ver! (*They fight.* CHOLULA *is defeated.*)

TLAXCALA: Te vencimos.

CHOLULA: Sí, pero con la ayuda de esos dioses blancos.

TLAXCALA: ¡Madre!

CHOLULA: ¡La tuya! (*They start to fight again.*)

MALINCHE: ¡Cállense! El señor Cortez quiere saber dónde está el oro.

CEMPOALA: ¿Oro?

CHOLULA: ¿Oro?

TLAXCALA: ¿Dónde está el oro?

CHOLULA: Pos allá en México con Moctezuma.

TLAXCALA: ¡Papas! ¡Tú te lo jambaste!

CHOLULA: ¡Pos, mira qué desgraciado! (*They start to fight.*)

MALINCHE: Shut up. El señor Cortez dice que descansen para poder derrotar a Moctezuma más pronto. El Moctezuma es el enemigo de todos nosotros. No le paguen las rentas. Los españoles son sus amigos verdaderos.

CHOLULA: ¡Viva Cortez! (*All cry out "¡Viva!"*)

PETE: Hey, you guys want some chicle? (*They all jump for some gum.*)

CHOLULA: Cortez . . .

CORTEZ: Yeah, boy?

CHOLULA: . . . is . . .

CORTEZ: Come on, boy, spit it out or I'll kick you from here to tequila.

CHOLULA: . . . my friend!

CORTEZ: Ah, my little brown brother.

ALL: Speech! Speech!

CORTEZ: We are gathered here on this . . . no that ain't going to cut it. Ask not what Cortez can do for Mexico, ask what Mexico can do for . . . no that ain't gonna cut it either. Yes, I got it, "My fellow Americans." (*Everyone cheers.*)

TLAXCALA: ¡Vamos a México! (*Exit.*)

CHOLULA: ¡Vamos a México! (*Exit.*)

CEMPOALA: ¡Vamos a México! (*Exit.*)

CORTEZ: Good Indians, good stupid Indians.

MALINCHE: ¡Vamos a México! (CORTEZ *and* MALINCHE *exit.*)

PETE: We're gonna get the gold! We're in the money! (*Music, drums, flutes, rattles.*)

PIEDRA: And so, in battle after battle with the gachupines, the feathered armies of Mexico were defeated by a few white men and their Indian allies. For weapons the Indians had bows and arrows, macanas and the atl-atl. The Spaniards had swords, muskets, cannons and the horse. While this was going on, Moctezuma could not decide what to do. All the conquered tribes were joining the gachupines.

MOCTEZUMA: ¡Indios montoneros! Unos por unos, me caen huangos, pero así juntos . . . ¡¡ay qué miedo!!

PIEDRA: What was bothering Moctezuma was that he could not decide if Cortez was Quetzalcóatl or not.

MOCTEZUMA: Si me lo echo y es un dios, ¡me friego! Y si no me lo echo, y es un hombre que nos viene a conquistar, ¡también me friego! ¡Chihuahua, qué hago!

CUAUHTEMOC: ¡Tío! ¡Vamos a darles en la madre! Alcabo, esos blancos no son dioses y mueren como hombres.

MOCTEZUMA: Cállate, Cuauhtémoc, nos echan al bote.

CUAUHTEMOC: Pos hay que hacer algo, porque ya mero llegan.

MOCTEZUMA: Vamos ami templo.

CUAUHTEMOC: Ahí te llevo.

PIEDRA: Finally the conquistadores arrived in the Valley of

Mexico, and this time they encountered the greatest defense of all.

CUAUHTEMOC: Simón, ¡yo Cuauhtémoc me los echo a todos con un dedo! (*Exit.*)

PIEDRA: But the gachupines were not alone. Cempoala, Tlaxcala, and Cholula had joined them in order to fight their most hated enemy, México. (*Spaniards and Indians enter marching.*)

ALL: (*Singing.*) Ya venimos de España, rum-bara-rum-bara-rum-bara-rum

Ya venimos de España, rum-bara-rum-bara-rum-bara-rum

Pa' matar a Moctezuma

Ay viruela, ay viruela

Ay viruela, ay viruela

CORTEZ: Column halt! Moctezuma, are you in there? Come on out, you punk. Tell him Malinche.

MALINCHE: Moctezuma, vale más que salgas y te rindas. Estos americanos tienen mucho poder para matarte. Vale más que salgas, mexicano idiota.

TLAXCALA: ¡En la madre! Ahora sí se va a poner bueno. ¡Arriba los españoles! (*Everyone yells arriba.*) ¡Abajo los mexicanos! (*Everyone yells "abajo."*)

CUAUHTEMOC: ¡Indios traicioneros! Ahora les voy a enseñar que nos obedezcan. (*He pops up.*)

MOCTEZUMA: Cállate, Cuauhtémoc, tal vez son dioses.

CUAUHTEMOC: ¿Cuáles dioses, tío? Mire, parecen bubble gum.

MOCTEZUMA: Cállate, Cuauhtémoc.

CUAUHTEMOC: Pero, tío, ¿a poco nos vamos a dejar que nos den en la torre?

MOCTEZUMA: Cállate, Cuauhtémoc.

CUAUHTEMOC: Pero, tío . . .

MOCTEZUMA: Shut up o te charapello.

PIEDRA: And Moctezuma, believing that Cortez was Quetzalcóatl, came down from his temple and greeted the white men with open arms.

INDIOS: (*Aghast.*) ¡El rey!

CORTEZ: ¡Amigo! (*Embraces* MOCTEZUMA. CORTEZ *stabs* MOCTEZUMA *and everyone gasps.*)

MOCTEZUMA: ¡Me mataron! (*He falls dead.*)

CUAUHTEMOC: ¡Tío! (*All the Indians yell "¡estamos libres!"*)

CORTEZ: Shut up! Shut up! I said shut up! I'm going to brand each and everyone of you so I can tell you apart.

TLAXCALA: ¿Qué dice ese güero?

MALINCHE: Que son indios estúpidos.

TLAXCALA: Huy, huy, ¿y tú, prieta?

MALINCHE: Yo no soy india. I'm Spanish. (*Everyone gives her a raspberry whistle.*)

TLAXCALA: Tírenle un hueso.

PIEDRA: After Moctezuma's death, Cuauhtémoc became chief.

CUAUHTEMOC: ¡Yo soy el chief! ¡Y aquí les viene Cuauhtémoc! (*He leaps down and starts to fight.*) ¡Ayyy! Palo, palo, bang, bang, zang, tas, tas, thud . . . (*Exit fighting.*)

PIEDRA: Cuauhtémoc defended México and cleared the capital of gachupines. Even so, the white men returned the following year, in 1521, and with the help of more Indians, thousands and thousands of them, they completed the conquest and total destruction of La Gran Tenochtitlán. Cuauhtémoc was taken to Guatemala to help in the search of more gold, and when he didn't tell the Spaniards where it was, they burned his feet and finally they hanged him.

CUAUHTEMOC: (*Reappears.*) Simón, pero nunca me rajé. Nosotros los mexicanos de la antigüedad, perdimos porque no estábamos unidos con nuestros carnales de la raza y porque creíamos que esos hombres blancos eran dioses poderosos y porque nunca nos pusimos abusados. ¡Ojalá que todavía no sea así! ¿Verdad, sol?

PIEDRA: ¡Simón! ¡Organícense raza!

No saco nada de la escuela

1969

First Performance: Centro Cultural Mexicano, St. John's
Church Fresno, California

Characters:

Francisco
Moctezuma (Monty)
Malcolm
Florence
Abraham
Grade School Teacher
Esperanza
College Professor
Nixon
Vato

*Elementary School. School Yard sounds: children playing,
shouting, laughing. Four kids come running out.* FLORENCE,
a white girl in pigtails and freckles; MALCOLM, *a black boy;*
then FRANCISCO *and* MOCTEZUMA, *two chicanitos.*

ALL: (*A cheer.*) Yeah! Ring around the rosey, pocket full of
posies, ashes, ashes, all fall down! Yeah! Let's do it again!
(FRANCISCO *has been watching from the side. He is*

grabbed by FLORENCE *and* MONTY, *and pulled into circle, trying to get in step.*) Ring around the rosey, pocket full of posies, ashes, ashes, we all fall down! (*Bell rings off stage.*)

FLORENCE: Oh! The bell! (*They jump to their places, and sit in two rows facing each other. Two on each side.*)

MONTY: Heh, look! Florence has a boyfriend! Florence has a boyfriend, y es un negro!

FLORENCE: No I don't. I don't have no boyfriend. (TEACHER *enters, short bowlegged, old, ugly. She wears a white mask and her feet stomp as she walks. She carries a huge pencil, two feet long, and a sign which she places on a stand at upstage center.*)

TEACHER: (*Mimicking writing on blackboard.*) Elementary A-B-C's. (*Students begin to throw paper wads across the room at one another.* TEACHER *turns, commands with high pitched voice.*) Children! I want those papers picked off the floor immediately! (*Students run to pick up papers. Then sit down.*) There now, that's better. (*Her version of cheerfulness.*) Good morning, class. (*Class begins to sing except for* FRANCISCO, *who looks at others, bewildered.* TEACHER *leads singing with her pencil.*)

ALL: Good morning to you, good morning to you, good morning dear teacher, good morning to you.

TEACHER: That's fine. Now for roll call. Florence.

FLORENCE: Here teacher.

TEACHER: Malcolm.

MALCOLM: Yeow.

TEACHER: Moc . . . Moc . . . (*She can't pronounce "Moctezuma."*) Ramírez!

MONTY: Here.

TEACHER: Francisco.

FRANCISCO: Aquí. (MONTY *raises* FRANCISCO's *hand.*)

TEACHER: Abraham.

MONTY: Teacher, teacher. He's outside. He's a crybaby.

(ABRAHAM *comes running out and runs across front stage, crying. He is dressed in cowboy boots, baseball cap on sideways, face is pale white with freckles.*)

TEACHER: (*Helps him.*) There, there now, dear, don't cry. I want you to sit right there. (*Points to* MONTY.)

ABRAHAM: Wah! I can't sit there, he's brown.

MONTY: No, I'm not. (*Rubs forearm trying to remove color.*)

TEACHER: (*Turns him around.*) Well, then I want you to sit right over there. (*Points towards* MALCOLM.)

ABRAHAM: Wah! I can't sit there, he's Black.

TEACHER: Well, then do you see that nice little white girl over there? (*Points to* FLORENCE.) Would you like to sit there?

ABRAHAM: (*Man's voice.*) Uh-huh!

TEACHER: Boy! (*Points to* MALCOLM.) You move. (ABRAHAM *sits next to* FLORENCE, MALCOLM *moves over by* MONTY *and* FRANCISCO. *They pantomine playing marbles.*)

TEACHER: Now, all rise for the flag salute. (*Sweetly.*) Stand up, Florence. Stand up, Abraham, dear. (*Turns to others.*) I said stand up! (MONTY, MALCOLM *and* FRANCISCO *jump up and begin flag salute.*)

ALL: I pledge allegiance to the flag . . . (ABRAHAM *sneaks behind the* TEACHER'*s back and pokes* FRANCISCO *in the behind.* FRANCISCO *thinks it was* MONTY *and hits him, pushing him into* MALCOLM. *They stand up straight again to continue and* ABRAHAM *sneaks over, again he pokes* FRANCISCO *who again hits* MONTY, *who again pushes into* MALCOLM. MALCOLM *points to* ABRAHAM. *All three then attack* ABRAHAM *and throw him to the ground.*)

TEACHER: (*Turns screaming.*) Class! For heaven's sake! (ABRAHAM, MONTY *and* FRANCISCO *run back to their seats.*) Did they hurt you Abraham, dear? (*Turns to* MONTY *and* FRANCISCO.) You should have more respect!

FRANCISCO: Pero, yo no hice nada.

TEACHER: Shut up! (FRANCISCO *cries.*) Shut up! I said shut up! (FRANCISCO *continues crying.* TEACHER *kicks him and he shuts up.* TEACHER *moves to center stage.*) And now for our elementary A, B, C's. Florence, you're first.

FLORENCE: Here's an apple, teacher. (*Hands* TEACHER *an apple.*)

TEACHER: Thank you, dear.

FLORENCE: (*Moves down stage center.*) A is for apple. B is for baby. And C is for candy. (*Pantomimes licking sucker and skips back to her seat giggling.*)

TEACHER: Very good! Now let's see who's next. Willie? (*She means* MALCOLM, *who sits daydreaming.*) Willie? (MALCOLM *does not respond.*) Willie! I meant you boy! (*Points at him.*)

MALCOLM: Teacher, my name ain't Willie. It's Malcolm.

TEACHER: It doesn't matter. It doesn't matter. Do your ABC's!

MALCOLM: A is for Alabama. B is for banjo and C is for cotton! (*Stamps foot, walks back to his seat. All the students are giggling.*)

TEACHER: Not bad at all, boy, not bad at all. Let's see. Who's next? Abraham dear? Say your ABC's.

ABRAHAM: A is for animal and B is for . . . black and brown! (*Points to* MONTY *and* FRANCISCO *and* MALCOLM.)

TEACHER: Oh! He's able to distinguish his colors. Go on.

ABRAHAM: And C is for . . . for . . .

TEACHER: It has a "kuh," "kuh" sound. (*Meaning cat.*)

ABRAHAM: Kill! (*Brightens up. Points to* FRANCISCO, MONTY *and* MALCOLM.)

TEACHER: Oh, no, we mustn't say those things in class.

ABRAHAM: (*Crying.*) I promise never to say it again. Teacher, look. (*Points upward.* TEACHER *looks and* ABRAHAM *spits on* FRANCISCO, MONTY *and* MALCOLM. *They start to get up but are interrupted by* TEACHER.)

TEACHER: Class! Did you all know that Abraham here was named after one of our most famous presidents? Mr. Abraham Lincoln — the man who freed the slaves!

ALL: (*Aghast.*) Gaw-leee!

TEACHER: After they were forced to pick cotton against their own free will.

ALL: Shame, shame, shame.

TEACHER: (*To* ABRAHAM.) Now, aren't you proud of your heritage?

ABRAHAM: A-huh. (*Laughing.*)

TEACHER: Of course, you are. Who's next. Moc . . . Moc . . . (*She can't pronounce his name.*) Ramírez!

MONTY: Yes, teacher?

TEACHER: How do you pronounce your name?

MONTY: Moctezuma.

TEACHER: What?

MONTY: Moctezuma.

TEACHER: Oh! What a funny name! (*She laughs and class joins her.* TEACHER *stomps foot and shuts them up.*) Class! (*To* MOCTEZUMA.) And what ever does it mean?

MONTY: He was an emperor in the times of the Indians. He was a Mexican like me.

TEACHER: Oh! You mean Montezuma.

MONTY: No, Moctezuma.

TEACHER: Montezuma.

MONTY: Moctezuma.

TEACHER: Montezuma!

MONTY: Moctezuma!

TEACHER: Montezuma! (*Begins to march up and down stage singing "The Marines Hymn."*) "From the halls of Monte-zoo-ma to the shore of Tripoli." (*Using her oversized pencil as a bayonet, she stabs* MONTY, *who falls forward with head and arms hanging.*) Now what's your name, boy? (*Lifts his head.*)

MONTY: Monty.

TEACHER: Do your ABC's.

MONTY: A is for airplane, B is for boat and C is for . . . ah, C is for . . . for cucaracha!

TEACHER: What!

MONTY: (*Crying.*) Cuca . . . caca qui qui.

TEACHER: (*Twisting his ear.*) What you meant to say was cock-a-roach, right?

MONTY: Sí.

TEACHER: What? (*Twists his ear even more.*)

MONTY: Yes!

TEACHER: Yes, what?

MONTY: Yes, teacher!

TEACHER: Sit down! (*He sits down crying.*) And shut up! Let's see who's next. Oh, yes, Francisco.

FRANCISCO: ¿Qué?

TEACHER: Oh! Another one that can't speak English! Why do they send these kids to me? You can't communicate with them. Is there anybody here that can speak Spanish?

MONTY: I can, teacher.

TEACHER: Tell him to do his ABC's.

MONTY: Dice que digas tu ABC's.

FRANCISCO: Dile que no las sabo en inglés, nomás en español.

MONTY: Teacher, he don't know how.

TEACHER: Oh, sit down! This has been a most trying day! Class dismissed . . . (*Students start to run out cheering.*) except (*They freeze.*) for Monty and Franky. (TEACHER *points to them. The rest of the class runs out.*)

MALCOLM: (*Offstage.*) You better give me that swing.

ABRAHAM: (*Offstage.*) No!

MALCOLM: (*Offstage.*) I'm gonna hit you.

ABRAHAM: (*Offstage.*) No. (*Slap is heard and then* ABRAHAM *wails.*)

TEACHER: (TEACHER, MONTY *and* FRANCISCO *freeze until after the above, then they being to move again.*) Now look, boy. Tell him his name is no longer Francisco, but Franky.

MONTY: Dice que tu nombre ya no es Francisco, es Franky.

FRANCISCO: No es Francisco . . . Panchito.

MONTY: Hey, teacher, he said his name is still Francisco. (FRANCISCO *punches him in the back.*)

TEACHER: Look boy, Francisco . . . no; Franky . . . yes.

FRANCISCO: No. Francisco.

TEACHER: Franky!

FRANCISCO: Francisco!

TEACHER: Franky!

FRANCISCO: Okay. (*As* TEACHER *begins to walk away to audience.*) Francisco.

TEACHER: It's Franky!

FRANCISCO: (*Grabs sign and throws it on the ground.*) Es Francisco, ya estufas.

TEACHER: Oh! You nasty boy! (*Beats him over the head twice.*) Remember the Alamo! (*Hits him again.*) And just for that, you don't pass.

MONTY: Teacher, teacher, do I pass? (*Picks up sign, and hands it to her.*)

TEACHER: I suppose so. You are learning to speak English. (*To audience.*) They shouldn't place these culturally deprived kids with the normal children. No, no, no. (*She leaves. Stomps out.* MONTY *begins to follow.*)

FRANCISCO: (*Getting up from floor.*) Oye, Moctezuma, ¿qué dijo esa vieja chaparra y panzona?

MONTY: Dijo que tú no pasaste. You don't pass.

FRANCISCO: ¿Y tú pasaste?

MONTY: Sure, I pass. I speak good English and, besides my name isn't Moctezuma anymore . . . it's Monty.

FRANCISCO: No, es Moctezuma.

MONTY: Monty.

FRANCISCO: Moctezuma.

MONTY: It's Monty. See, you stupid? You never learn. (*Sticks his tongue out at him and leaves.*)

FRANCISCO: (*Crying.*) Entonces dile a tu teacher que coma chet! (*Leaves crying.*)

High School. Scene begins with same stand at center stage. High school teacher, male, grey business suit, white mask. Walks across stage. Places high school sign on board.

STUDENTS: (*Backstage, singing.*) Oh hail to thee, our Alma Mater, we'll always hold you dear. (*Then a cheer.*) Rah, rah, sis boom bah! Sock it to them, sock it to them! (FLORENCE *enters stage right.* ABRAHAM *enters stage left. His neck has a reddish tinge. He tries to hug* FLORENCE *and is pushed away. He tries again and is pushed away.* FLORENCE *continues walking.*)

ABRAHAM: Where you going?

FLORENCE: To class.

ABRAHAM: What do you mean to class? I thought we were going steady.

FLORENCE: We were going steady.

ABRAHAM: (*Mimicking her.*) What do you mean "We were going steady?"

FLORENCE: That's right. I saw you walking with that new girl, Esperanza.

ABRAHAM: That Mexican chick? Aw, you know what I want from her. Besides, you're the only girl I love. I'll even get down on my knees for you. (*Falls on knees.*)

FLORENCE: Oh! Abe, don't be ridiculous, get up.

ABRAHAM: (*Getting up.*) Does that mean we're still going steady?

FLORENCE: I guess so.

ABRAHAM: Hot dog! (*From stage right* FRANCISCO *enters wearing dark glasses and strutting like a vato loco.* ABRAHAM *to* FLORENCE.) See that spic over there? Just to show you how much I love you, I'm gonna kick his butt!

FLORENCE: Oh, Abe, you can't be racist!

ABRAHAM: Get out of my way. (*Does warm up exercises like a boxer.* FRANCISCO *has been watching him all along and has a knife in his hand, hidden behind his back so that it is not visible.*) Heh, greaser, spic!

FRANCISCO: (*Calmly.*) You talking to me, bato?

ABRAHAM: You want some beef? (*Raises his fists.*)

FRANCISCO: (*To audience.*) Este vato quiere pedo. ¿Cómo la ven? ¡Pos que le ponga! (*Pulls out a knife and goes after* ABRAHAM.)

ABRAHAM: (*Backing up.*) Heh, wait a minute! I didn't mean it. I was only fooling. I . . . (FRANCISCO *thrusts knife toward* ABRAHAM. FLORENCE *steps in between and stops the knife by holding* FRANCISCO's *arm. Action freezes. From stage right* MALCOLM *jumps in and struts downstage. He wears a do rag on his head, and sun glasses. He bops around, snapping his fingers; walks up to* FRAN-CISCO *and* ABRAHAM; *looks at knife, feels the blade and walks away as if nothing is happening. From stage right,* MONTY *enters with his arm around* ESPERANZA "HOPI." *He runs up to* MALCOLM.)

MONTY: Hey, man, what's going on here?

MALCOLM: Say, baby, I don't know. I just don't get into these things. (*Moves away.*)

MONTY: (*Stops him.*) Hey, man, I said what's going on here?

MALCOLM: And I said I don't get into these things! What's the matter with you? Don't you understand? Don't you speak English?

MONTY: (*Angered.*) You think you're better than me, huh? (MONTY *grabs* MALCOLM *by the throat, and* MAL-COLM *grabs him back. They start choking each other.* TEACHER *enters stage center and observes the fight.*)

MONTY: Nigger!

MALCOLM: Greaser!

MONTY: Spic!

MONTY: Coon!

ESPERANZA: Oh, Monty, Monty!

TEACHER: Okay, that's enough. Cut it out, boys! We can settle this after school in the gym. We might even charge admission. Everyone to your seats. (MONTY *and* MALCOLM *separate.* FRANCISCO *puts his knife away and all move back to their seats.*)

TEACHER: Now, before we begin, I want to know who started that fight.

ABRAHAM: (*Innocently.*) Mr. White? He did, Sir.

FRANCISCO: (*Stands up.*) I didn't start anything. He insulted me!

ABRAHAM: Who you going to believe, him or me? Besides, he pulled a knife.

TEACHER: (*To* FRANCISCO.) You did what? Get to the Principal's office immediately!

FRANCISCO: Orale, but you know what? This is the last time I'm going to the Principal's office for something like this. (*Exits mumbling.*) Me la vas a pagar, ese, qué te crees.

TEACHER: I don't understand that boy. And he's one of the school's best athletes. (*Opens mouth, sudden realization. Runs to exit, shouts after* FRANCISCO.) Don't forget to show up for baseball practice. The school needs you.

FLORENCE: (*Stands.*) Mr. White? I refuse to sit next to Abraham. He's a liar!

TEACHER: (*Stands next to* ABRAHAM.) Why, Florence, Abe here is the son of one of our best grower families.

FLORENCE: Well, I don't care if you believe me or not. But I refuse to sit next to a liar. (*Gives* ABRAHAM *his ring.*) And here's your ring!

TEACHER: All right, sit over here. (FLORENCE *moves across stage and sits next to* ESPERANZA. FRANCISCO *comes strutting in, whistling.*) I thought I told you to go to the Principal's office.

FRANCISCO: I did, man.

TEACHER: What did he say?

FRANCISCO: He told me not to beat on anymore of his gabachitos. (*Taps* ABRAHAM *on the head.*)

TEACHER: (*Angered.*) All right, sit over there. (*Indicates a spot beside* FLORENCE.) And you . . . (*To* ESPERANZA.) over here.

ESPERANZA: (*Stops beside* FRANCISCO *at center stage.*) You rotten pachuco. (*She sits besides* ABRAHAM.)

FRANCISCO: Uh que la . . . esta ruca, man. (*He sits besides* FLORENCE.)

TEACHER: Now, class, before we begin our high school reports, I'd like to introduce a new student. Her name is Esperanza Espinoza. (*He gives the pronunciation of her name with an Italian inflection.*) It sounds Italian, I know, but I think she's Mexican-American. Isn't that right, dear?

ESPERANZA: (*Self-consciously rising.*) No, my parents were, but I'm Hawaiian. And you can just call me Hopi.

TEACHER: That's fine, Hopi. Now for our high school reports. Florence, you're first.

FLORENCE: (*Drumbeats.* FLORENCE *walks to center stage, swaying hips like a stripper.*) A is for achievement. B is for betterment. And C is for (*Bump and grind.*) college! (*More drumbeats as she walks back to her seat.*)

TEACHER: (*Impressed.*) Well! It's good to see that you're thinking of your future. Let's see who's next. Oh yes, Willie.

MALCOLM: (*Hopes to his feet.*) I told you, man, my name ain't Willie. It's Malcolm!

TEACHER: All right, you perfectionist! Get up there and give your report.

MALCOLM: (*Struts to center stage. He begins to snap his fingers, setting a rhythm. Everybody joins in.*) A is for africa. B is for black like me. And C is for community like black ghetto.

ALL: (*Still snapping to rhythm.*) My goodness, Willie, you sure got rhythm. But then after all, all you people do. (*Three final snaps.*)

TEACHER: Now then, Willie, about your report. The first two pages were fine, but that last part about the ghetto . . . don't you think it needs some improvement?

MALCOLM: You're telling me! Don't you think we know it?

TEACHER: Okay, that's a good C minus. Back to your seat. (MALCOLM *sits down.*) Abraham, up front!

ABRAHAM: Jabol mein fuehrer! (*Stomps to center stage.*) A is for America: Love or leave it! (FRANCISCO *and* MALCOLM *stand up to leave.*)

TEACHER: Heh, you two! (*Motions for them to sit down.*)

ABRAHAM: B is for better: Better dead than red. And C is for kill, kill, kill! As in the United States Marine Corps. (*Snaps to attention.*)

TEACHER: (*Marches up like a Marine.*) Very good, Abraham!

ABRAHAM: (*Saluting.*) Thank you, sir.

TEACHER: That's an A plus, Abraham!

ABRAHAM: What did you expect, sir?

TEACHER: Dismissed! (ABRAHAM *marches back to seat.*) Monty, up front!

MONTY: Yes, sir! (*Marches sloppily to stage center. Salutes and freezes.*)

TEACHER: (*With contempt.*) Cut that out, and give your report.

MONTY: A is for American. B is for beautiful, like America the Beautiful. And C is for country, like God bless this beautiful American country! Ooooh, I love it. (*He falls to his knees, kisses the floor.*)

TEACHER: (*Grabs* MONTY *by the collar like a dog.*) Here, have a dog biscuit. (MONTY *scarfs up imaginary dog biscuit, then is led back to his seat on all fours by* TEACHER.) Now, who's next? Oh yes, Hopi.

ESPERANZA: (*Rises prissily, goes to center stage.*) A is for Avon, as in "Ding dong, Avon calling." B is for burgers, which I love, and beans, which I hate! (*Sneers at* FRANCISCO.) And C is for can't as in "I can't speak Spanish." And we have a new Buick Riviera, and my sister goes to the University of California, and we live in a tract home . . .

TEACHER: (*Leading her back to her seat.*) Yes, dear! Just fine!

ESPERANZA: Really, really we do!

TEACHER: I believe you. That deserves a bean . . . uh, I mean B plus. (*Pause.*) Now let's hear from . . . Franky?

FRANCISCO: Yeah, Teach?

TEACHER: What do you mean "yeah, Teach?" You know my name is Mr. White.

FRANCISCO: I know what you name is, ese. But you seem to forget that my name is Francisco, loco.

TEACHER: Get up and give your report, you hoodlum.

FRANCISCO: Orale, ese vato, llévatela suave. (*Moves to center stage.*) A is for amor, como amor de mi raza.

TEACHER: What!

FRANCISCO: B is for barrio como where the raza lives. (TEACHER *growls.*) And C is carnalismo.

TEACHER: (*Heated.*) How many times have I told you about speaking Spanish in my classroom?! Now what did you say?

FRANCISCO: Carnalismo.

TEACHER: (*At the limit of his patience.*) And what does that mean?

FRANCISCO: Brotherhood.

TEACHER: (*Blows up.*) Get out!!

FRANCISCO: Why? I was only speaking my language. I'm a Chicano, ¿que no?

TEACHER: Because I don't understand you, and the rest of the class doesn't understand you.

FRANCISCO: So what? When I was small, I didn't understand English, and you kept flunking me and flunking me instead of teaching me.

TEACHER: You are permanently expelled from this high school!

FRANCISCO: Big deal! You call yourself a teacher! I can communicate in two languages. You can only communicate in one. Who's the teacher, Teach? (*Starts to exit.*)

MONTY: We're not all like that, teacher.

FRANCISCO: ¡Tú te me callas! (*Pushes* MONTY *aside and exits.*)

TEACHER: That's the last straw! A is for attention. B is for brats like that. And C is for cut out. High school dismissed! (TEACHER *exits, taking high school sign with him.* MALCOLM *exits also at opposite side of stage.* ABRAHAM, FLORENCE, ESPERANZA *and* MONTY *rise, facing each other.*)

MONTY: (*Looking at* FLORENCE.) Oh, Hopi?

ESPERANZA: (*Looking at* ABRAHAM.) Yes?

ABRAHAM: (*Looking at* ESPERANZA.) Oh, Flo?

FLORENCE: (*Looking at* MONTY.) Yeah?

ABRAHAM *and* MONTY: (*Together.*) Do you wanna break up?

FLORENCE *and* ESPERANZA: (*Together.*) Yeah! (MONTY *takes* FLORENCE *by the arm;* ABRAHAM *takes* ESPERANZA.

MONTY: Oh boy, let's go to a party.

ABRAHAM: Let's go to a fiesta. (*All exit.*)

State College. Backstage sounds: Police siren, shouts of "pigs off campus!" College PROFESSOR *enters and places sign on stand. It reads, "State College."* FRANCISCO *enters pushing a broom.*

FRANCISCO: Oh, professor?

PROFESSOR: Yes?

FRANCISCO: I want to go to college.

PROFESSOR: Didn't you drop out of high school?

FRANCISCO: Simón, but I still want to go to college. I want to educate myself.

PROFESSOR: Well, that's tough. (*Exits.*)

FRANCISCO: Pos, mira, qué jijo . . . (*Swings broom.* FLORENCE *enters followed by* MONTY. FRANCISCO *freezes.*)

FLORENCE: Guess what, folks? Monty and I are living together. Isn't that right, Monty?

MONTY: That's right, baby. Just me and you.

FLORENCE: Do you love me, Monty?

MONTY: Oh, you know I do.

FLORENCE: Then, come to momma!

MONTY: Ay mamasota, una gabacha! (*He runs over to her and begins to kiss her passionately.*)

FLORENCE: (*Swooning.*) Oh, you Latin lovers.

MONTY: (*Suddenly peeved.*) Latin lovers? Your people have been oppressing my people for 150 years!

FLORENCE: Yes, Monty!

MONTY: You gabachas are all alike!

FLORENCE: (*The guilty liberal.*) Oh yes, Monty!

MONTY: And that's why I'm going to give it to you! (*Rolls up his sleeve, clenches fist.*) Right between the you-know-what. (*Grabs her and begins to kiss her again passionately.*) ¡Viva Zapata! (*Makes out again.*) ¡Viva Villa! (*Raises fist.*) ¡Viva la Revolución! (*Wraps a leg around her. Kisses her. Then falls to the floor exhausted.*)

FLORENCE: (*Sitting on his back.*) Oh, Monty. You do that so well.

MONTY: (*Puffing underneath.*) Shut up. While my people are starving in the barrio, your people are sitting fat and reech.

FLORENCE: Reech?

MONTY: Rich! Rich, you beech. Oh, my accent sleeped . . . slopped, sloped! What am I saying?

FLORENCE: (*Noticing* FRANCISCO.) Monty, look, a chicken-o.

MONTY: A what?

FLORENCE: A Mexican-American?

MONTY: A what?

FLORENCE: An American of Mexican descent?

MONTY: I'm going to give you one more chance. I'm going to spell it out for you. (*Spells out C-H-I-C-A-N-O in the air.*) What's this?

FLORENCE: (*Reading his movements.*) C!

MONTY: And this and this? (*H and I.*)

FLORENCE: C-H-I . . . Chic! Chica . . . oh, Chicano! Chicano! (*Jumps up and down.*)

MONTY: Good! Now get out. And don't come back until I call you. (FLORENCE *exits.*) 'Cause this is a job for . . . Super-macho! (*Approaches* FRANCISCO. *Anglo accent to his Spanish.*) ¿Qué-húbole, esay bato loco? Heh, don't I know you?

FRANCISCO: ¿Qué nuevas?

MONTY: Isn't your name Francisco?

FRANCISCO: Simón.

MONTY: You're wanted.

FRANCISCO: No, I'm not! (*Begins to run across stage.*)

MONTY: For our program. (*Stops* FRANCISCO.)

FRANCISCO: What program?

FLORENCE: (*Sticking her head out from backstage.*) Now Monty?

MONTY: No, not yet. (*Turns to* FRANCISCO.) Hey, man, you know la raza is getting together! You know we have 300 years of Chicano culture? You know our women are beautiful?! Just look at them, mamasotas!

FRANCISCO: Simón, están a toda madre.

MONTY: Pero primero necesitamos unos cuantos gritos como los meros machos. Mira, fíjate, ¡Que viva la raza! (FRAN-CISCO *repeats.*) ¡Que viva la huelga! (FRANCISCO *repeats.*)

FLORENCE: (*Enters.*) Look, Monty, I'm getting tired of waiting, godamit!

MONTY: (*Turns to* FLORENCE.) Okay, just wait a minute. Just one more. (*Turns to* FRANCISCO.) Uno más pero éste con muchos tú sabes qué, ¿eh? ¡Que viva la revolución!

FRANCISCO: ¿La revolución . . . ? (*Looks at* FLORENCE.) Pos que viva, y a comenzar con esa gabacha, jija de . . .

MONTY: Hey, wait a minute, man. That's not where it's at, bato.

81

This is what you call "universal love." I don't think you're
ready for college. (FLORENCE *jumps on* MONTY *'s back.*)
And when you are, come look for me up at the Mexican
Opportunity Commission Organization: MOCO. And I'm
the Head Moco. Chicano Power, carnal! (*Exits.*)

FRANCISCO: (*To audience.*) No, hombre, está más mocoso
que la . . . (HOPI *and* ABRAHAM *enter stage left.* ABRA-
HAM *is wearing at ten gallon hat.*)

ESPERANZA: Guess what, folks? Abraham and I are engaged.
Isn't that right, Abraham?

ABRAHAM: That's right, baby. Just me and you. (*He leans her
over to kiss her.*)

ESPERANZA: (*Snapping back up. To* FRANCISCO.) What are
you looking at?

FRANCISCO: Oh! Esperanza, ¿no te acuerdas de mí?

ESPERANZA: My name is Hopi.

FRANCISCO: Orale, esa, no te . . .

ABRAHAM: Is that Mexican bothering you?

ESPERANZA: Just ignore him, sugar plum, just ignore him.
(*They move stage right.*) ABRAHAM: Do you know that
my dad owns 200,00 acres of lettuce in the Salinas Valley?

ESPERANZA: Really!

ABRAHAM: And he has 200 dumb Mexicans just like him
working for him.

ESPERANZA: Really!

ABRAHAM: My daddy's a genius!

ESPERANZA: Oh! You're so smart! You're so intelligent! Oh,
you white god, you! (*Bows falling on her knees in worship.*)

ABRAHAM: Shucks. You don't have to do that. Why, you
remind me of a little brown squaw my grandpappy used to
have.

ESPERANZA: Squaw! (*Getting up in anger.*)

ABRAHAM: Don't get mad, my little taco. My little tamale. My
little frijol. (*Pronounced free hole.*)

FRANCISCO: Free hole?

ABRAHAM: Besides, I've got a surprise for you. Why, just the other day my pappy made me president.

ESPERANZA: President?

ABRAHAM: President!

ESPERANZA: Of the company?

ABRAHAM: Of the Future Farmers of America.

ESPERANZA: (*Disappointed.*) Oh, Abraham.

FRANCISCO: (*Laughing, moves up to* HOPI.) ¿Oyes, por eso venistes al colegio? ¿A toparte con un pendejo?

ESPERANZA: Well, at least he's not out on the corner pushing dope.

ABRAHAM: You Mexicans ought to be out in the fields.

ESPERANZA: (*To* ABRAHAM.) You tell him, sugar.

FRANCISCO: That's all you think I can do, huh? Well I'm gonna go to college on the E.O.P. program!

ESPERANZA: Look. I made it through college without any assistance. I don't see why you can't.

FRANCISCO: (*Mimics her.*) I made it through college . . . (PROFESSOR *enters stage center,* MONTY *and* FLORENCE *enter stage right.*)

PROFESSOR: Ladies and gentlemen, can we prepare for our college seminar? (*Spots* FRANCISCO.) Aren't you the custodian?

FRANCISCO: Yes, but, a . . . Monty wants to talk to you.

MONTY: Oh, sir, we thought we might be able to get him in under MOCO, you know, Mexican Opportunity Commission Organization?

PROFESSOR: Now look, Monty, we got you in here and unless you want to be out, get back into your place. (*To* FRANCISCO.) No, I'm sorry, there's no room. No room! (*Pushes him out.*)

FRANCISCO: I want to go to college!

PROFESSOR: These students, they don't understand. (*To audience.*) They don't realize that there is no room in our college, no room at all. In this college there is not room for one more

83

student. Not one more minority student. (MALCOLM *enters stage right wearing a black shirt, black leather jacket and black beret. He is carrying a rifle.* ABRAHAM *begins to shake and points at him.*)

PROFESSOR: (*To* ABRAHAM.) I'll handle it. (*Moves over to* MALCOLM.) Pardon me, boy, but are you registered? (MALCOLM *cocks rifle,* PROFESSOR *looks at rifle chamber, looks at* MALCOLM, *looks at audience.*) He's registered.

ALL: He's registered.

FRANCISCO: (*Peeking back in.*) ¿Vistes eso, Moctezuma?

PROFESSOR: No, no, out! Out! (MOCTEZUMA *helps* PROFESSOR *push* FRANCISCO *out.*)

MONTY: (*Pushes him out.*) I'll see that it doesn't happen again, sir.

PROFESSOR: Well, see that it doesn't. Now class, in order to qualify for graduation, you must deliver one final report. And it must be concise, logical and have conviction. Miss Florence, you're first.

FLORENCE: A is for anti as in anti-war. B is for Berkeley as in anti-war Berkeley. And C is for chick as in anti-war Berkeley chick.

PROFESSOR: Well, that was a very personal and revealing account, Miss Florence, and that should qualify for . . .

ABRAHAM: That stunk! And if you pass her, I'll have your job. Remember, you are working for my daddy!

MONTY: Oh, sir, please give her one more chance.

PROFESSOR: Yes, just get back to your seat, Monty. I was about to say that it lacked conviction. Try again, Miss Florence. (*Stands next to her.*)

FLORENCE: A is for adult.

PROFESSOR: A-huh.

FLORENCE: B is for become, as to become an adult.

PROFESSOR: It happens to the best of us.

FLORENCE: And C is for cop-out, as to become an adult and

cop-out.

PROFESSOR: That is the American way, Miss Florence. You will graduate! Let's see who's next . . . Malcolm.

MALCOLM: (*Moves forward menacingly.*) A is for Afro, as in Afro-American. B is for Black, as in Afro-American Black Panther. And C is for Cleaver, Eldridge Cleaver, Afro-American Black Panther! (*Gives panther salute.*)

PROFESSOR: Well, I see the logic, but I don't like it.

MALCOLM: Good, that's the way we want it!

PROFESSOR: All right! All right! You'll graduate.

ABRAHAM: He graduates? (*He begins to pantomime different ways of killing* MALCOLM. *Machine gun, grenades, airplane and finally builds a rocket.*) A is for anti. (*Puts first stage of missile.*) B is for ballistic. (*Builds second stage.*) And M is for missile. (*Puts final stage on missile. During the above,* MALCOLM *has just been standing, cool and collected. Everybody but* MALCOLM *begins the countdown.*)

ALL: 5-4-3-2-1 Fire! (*They make whistling noise of a rocket in the air. As the rocket lands with a loud noise,* MALCOLM *turns around and points gun at* ABRAHAM.)

ABRAHAM: (*Scared like a boy.*) A is for animal. B is for back off. And C is for coward, Mama! (*Exits.*)

PROFESSOR: Abraham, come back! (FRANCISCO *enters stage left dressed as a brown beret with rifle in hand.*)

FRANCISCO: ¿Ya ves, Moctezuma? (MONTY *tries to push him out, but is thrown back.*) ¡Un lado!

PROFESSOR: Just a minute! Just a minute! (*To* FRANCISCO.) You want to go to college? What are your qualifications?

FRANCISCO: My qualifications? Pos, mira que jijo de . . . (*Pulls back rifle into position to hit* TEACHER *from the front and* MALCOLM *pokes his gun at his back. They freeze and* ESPERANZA *walks over and moves around* FRANCISCO, *checking him out. She moves back to her place.*)

PROFESSOR: (*Jumps up and they unfreeze.*) All right, you're in!

FRANCISCO: Where do I sit?

PROFESSOR: Over there! (*Frantically*.) This is getting out of hand. Monty, Monty, my boy, your report.

MONTY: A is for American like a Mexican-American.

PROFESSOR: Wonderful!

MONTY: And B is for bright, like a bright Mexican-American.

PROFESSOR: Great! Great!

MONTY: And C is for comprado like a bright, Mexican-American comprado.

PROFESSOR: Bought and sold! Monty, my boy, you will graduate. Congratulations! And as you go forward into this great society, I want you to remember one thing. (*Points forward*.) I want you always to move forward, move forward in that great American tradition. (MONTY *has been looking to where the* PROFESSOR *has been pointing, gets scared and sneaks off to his place, moving backward*.) Forever forward. (*Looks around when he realizes that* MONTY *has left*.) Monty! Monty! (*Getting hysterical*.) Oh! This is getting out of hand! Out of hand! Let's see. Oh, yes, Hopi?

ESPERANZA: (*She has been talking to* FRANCISCO *and now has her arms around his neck*.) Who?

PROFESSOR: (*Scared*.) Hopi?

ESPERANZA: My name is Esperanza, you marrano!

PROFESSOR: Your report, please.

ESPERANZA: Orale, llévatela suave. (*Walks pachuca fashion to center stage*.) A is for action, as in acción social. B is for batos, as in acción social de batos. And C is for Chicana as in Acción Social de Batos y Chicanas. (FRANCISCO *lets out with a grito*.)

FRANCISCO: ¿Y ahora qué dices, Moctezuma?

PROFESSOR: All right, Francisco, your report.

FRANCISCO: Hey, wait a minute, man. I just got in here.

MONTY: What's the matter? Can't do it, huh?

PROFESSOR: (*Regaining a sense of authority*.) Is that your problem, boy, can't you do it?

FRANCISCO: Yes, I can! And don't call me boy!

PROFESSOR: (*Cringes in fear again.*) Fine, fine.

FRANCISCO: A is for advanced, as the advanced culture of Indigenous American Aztlán. B is for bronce as in the advanced culture of Indigenous American Aztlán, which brought bronze civilization to the Western Hemisphere. And C is for century, as the advanced culture of Indigenous American Aztlán, which brought bronze civilization to the Western Hemisphere and which, moreover, will create el nuevo hombre in the twenty-first century, El Chicano. Give me my diploma.

PROFESSOR: Just a minute, hold it right there! (*Goes to side and grabs book.*) I have here in my hand the book of American knowledge. There is nothing in here about As-ta-lan, nothing in here about Chicken-o. In fact there is nothing in here about nothing and, as you can see, (*Turns book towards the audience, there is a dollar sign printed on page.*) this is the honest truth which is close to all of our American hearts. No, I'm sorry, but under the circumstances, I don't think that you will (FRANCISCO *has gun in* PROFESSOR'*s face and* MALCOLM *puts his rifle to his back.*) be here next year, because you will graduate. (MALCOLM *and* FRANCISCO *move to their places.*) And now, students, line up for that golden moment, graduation! And here to present the awards on this fine day is none other than that great statesman, that golden-mouthed orator, that old grape sucker himself, the President of the United States, Mr. Richard Nixon. (NIXON *moves in from stage right, he is wearing cap and gown, giving peace symbol. Shakes hands with* PROFESSOR.) A few words, please, Mr. President.

NIXON: I'd like to say just three things today, only three. First, don't forget that great American dollar which put you through college. (*Applause.*) Second, always kiss ass; and third, eat plenty of Salinas scab lettuce!

PROFESSOR: Thank you, Mr. President. Now, if you'll just step this way, we shall begin the awards. First, we have Miss Florence, a fine girl. (FLORENCE *moves to centerstage, receives diploma.* NIXON *places a graduation cap on her head. Cap comes with white hood, which covers her head completely. She moves back to her place.*) Next we have, Monty. Good boy. (MONTY *walks up and kisses the* PRESIDENT'*s hand. Then he places cap over his own head, goes back to his place.*) Next is Willie.

PRESIDENT: Here we are, Willie.

MALCOLM: (*Takes diploma.*) My name is Malcolm, you white mutha. (PRESIDENT *and* PROFESSOR *duck.*)

PRESIDENT: And here's your white bag.

MALCOLM: I don't need that.

PROFESSOR: But what are you going to do without it?

MALCOLM: You're going to find out. (*He walks to stage right and whistles.*) Come here, baby. (FLORENCE *takes off her cap, moves to center stage, throws cap on floor, walks off stage with* MALCOLM.)

PRESIDENT: A militant!

PROFESSOR: That's okay. There's a whole lot of them that aren't. Next we have Francisco. (FRANCISCO *moves up, takes diploma, moves quickly back to his place.* PRESIDENT *tries to put cap on him, misses and almost falls on* ESPERANZA. *He backs off cautiously.*)

PRESIDENT: Speedy, these Mexicans. Fast!

PROFESSOR: Next, we have Esperanza. (*She moves to center stage, takes diploma.*)

PRESIDENT: And here's your white bag.

ESPERANZA: I don't need your white bag!

PRESIDENT: But you can't exist in our society without me.

PROFESSOR: What are you going to do without your white bag? (*From audience someone gets up and yells, "Hey, I want to go to college."*)

ESPERANZA: That's what I'm going to do. I'm going to help

my carnales get into college.

BATO: ¡Ayúdenme! (*Runs toward stage.*)

PROFESSOR: No! (FRANCISCO *and* ESPERANZA *try to help* BATO *from audience. There's tug of war.*)

BATO: ¡Sí! (*With* FRANCISCO *and* ESPERANZA.)

PROFESSOR: No!

BATO: ¡Sí!

PROFESSOR: No!

BATO: ¡Sí! (*Jumps up onstage, pushing* PROFESSOR *back.* BATO *waves to audience and yells.*) Orale, I made it into college. (*Gives Chicano handsake to* FRANCISCO *and* ESPERANZA.)

PRESIDENT: Well, I can see that my job here is done. I shall now take my students, student . . . into the great white world. Right face! Forward march! (*Exits stage right followed by* MONTY.)

FRANCISCO: ¡Moctezuma! ¡Quédate con tu raza!

ESPERANZA: Ah, let him go. There's more where he came from.

FRANCISCO: ¡Pos, que le pongan! (*Students start coming in from all sides of stage, everyone starts pointing at* PROFESSOR *yelling.*) Teach us! Teach us!

PROFESSOR: Just a minute. Just a minute. (*To audience.*) So many brown faces, brown minds, brown ideas, what is this? A chocolate factory? (*Everybody jumps at him.*) I'm going to a college where they understand. Where they appreciate good white professors, where there won't be any Chicanos . . . like Fresno State College. President Baxter, help!!! (*Exits stage right. Everybody starts looking for change.* BATO *begins to take collection.*)

FRANCISCO: ¿Colecta, para qué?

FIRST NEW STUDENT: La birria.

SECOND NEW STUDENT: La mota.

THIRD NEW STUDENT: El wine.

FRANCISCO: Pos, ¿no están bien, calabazas? Estamos en

colegio. Hay que aprender de nuestra cultura, nuestra raza, de Aztlán.

BATO: (*Turns to next student.*) But who's going to teach us? (*They move on down the line asking each other the same question.*)

ESPERANZA: (*Last in line, asks* FRANCISCO.) Who's going to teach us?

FRANCISCO: Who's going to teach us?

ALL: Our own people! (*They point at audience.*)

FRANCISCO: ¿Entonces, qué se dice? ¡Viva . . .!

ALL: ¡La raza!

FRANCISCO: ¡Viva!

ALL: ¡La huelga!

FRANCISCO: ¡Chicano!

ALL: Power! (*Actors get audience to shout "Chicano power." Then all sing "bella ciao.*")

The Militants

1969

Characters

Dr. Bolillo
Chicano #1
Chicano #2

A Gabacho enters and approachoes the microphone.

GABACHO: Good evening, ladies and gentlemen, I am Dr. Bolillo and I am here to welcome you to the University of California's lecture series. We are very pleased to bring you an especially delightful speaker this evening. He is a well known member of the Mexican-American community, a rapper and most importantly, a militant. He has kindly consented to come here tonight and "tell it like it is." It is with great pleasure, therefore, that I now introduce this young man who is going to come out here and "sock it to us." His name is Benjamin Dejo — Ben Dejo! Let's give him a big hand. (*Applause.*) Ben? (*Two Chicano militants enter. The* GABACHO *only sees one of them. He shakes his hand. The other militant taps him on the shoulder. Turning.*) Oh, another one. Well, there must be some mistake. We only asked for one. Which one of you is Ben Dejo? (*Both militants step forward.*) I see. Okay. Well, sit down while

we settle this. (*They sit down.*) Will the real militant Ben
Dejo please rise? (*Both rise.*) Gentlemen, I tell you what we
are going to do. We're going to allow you both to speak. So
that means that you are going to have to be Chicano #1 and
you, Chicano #2. Okay? (*Militants agree.*) The floor is
yours.

CHICANO #1: (*To* CHICANO #2.) Orale, ese, vamos a darles en
la madre, ¿eh?

CHICANO #2: That's together, sock it to 'em. (*They do the chi-
cano handshake.*)

CHICANO #1: (*At the microphone.*) Señoras y señores, ladies
and gentlemen, and Anglos.

GABACHO: (*From his chair.*) Oh, that was good. Good start!

CHICANO #1: I didn't come here tonight to beat around the
bush, so I'm not going to do it. I come here to tell you the
truth. Our people are starving in the barrios and slaving in
the fields for starvation wages. You know how come?
Because of the oppression and economic exploitation that
Anglo growers and businessmen have imposed upon us. So
long as these damn Anglos have all the economic and politi-
cal power to control us, we're going to be at the bottom of
the barrel. We've got to get together and organize. Unite!
Strike! We've got to march to Sacramento like César
Chávez! Demand better wages, better schools, better jobs.
¡Viva la huelga! ¡Viva la causa!

CHICANO #2: ¡Raza! I've come here tonight to tell you where
it's at. I agree with everything the carnal here had to say, but
now I'm going to tell you what's really happening. Our
Raza is starving in the barrios and slaving in the fields for
starvation wages. You know how come? Because of the
oppression and economic exploitation of this gringo sitting
right here! This gabacho!

GABACHO: That's me. I admit it. (*Beats his chest.*)

CHICANO #2: My non-violent carnal means well, but we gotta
do more than march! We've got to drive the gabacho out of

the barrio! ¡Viva la huelga! ¡Viva la causa! ¡Viva la raza!
GABACHO: ¡Viva! Sock it to me, baby!
CHICANO #1: Okay. I agree with everything my carnal had to
say, only a lot more. When I said march to Sacramento, that
didn't mean I'm non-violent. Non-violence works, sure, but
to a limit. What my carnal over there was afriad to say was
that we need guns! Simón, I'm not afraid to say it! ¡Armas!
¡Rifles! ¡Pistolas! We've got to drive the gabacho out of the
barrios with guns! ¡Viva la huelga! ¡Viva la cuasa! ¡Viva la
raza! ¡Viva la Revolución!
CHICANO #2: Revolución, sure! That's together. But, baby, let
me tell you that guns ain't the only thing that's going to
make a revolucion! The trouble with you is that you've lost
contact with the barrio! Look at our history, at Pancho Villa,
Emiliano Zapata — they had what it takes! And what was
that? What is that pair of something every macho has in the
barrio? That makes every real revolutionary willing to die
at any moment? Like me, I'm willing to die! Any pigs in
the audience? Kill me! Go on, I'm ready! Kill me! I'm not
afraid, because I know what it takes: a good pair of . . .
bigotes! ¡Viva la huelga! ¡Viva la Causa! ¡Viva la raza!
¡Viva la revolución! ¡Vivan los bigotes!!!
CHICANO #1: What bigotes, ese, you can't even grow one! At
least I got an excuse. If I've lost contact with the barrio, it's
because I'm part of the vanguard. We're more Chicano than
anybody in the Southwest, I mean, Aztlán! We think,
breathe, feel, eat and dress Chicano! See this shirt! It's a
Chicano shirt. Camisas, manlisas! That's where it's at!
¡Viva la raza! ¡Viva la revolucion! ¡Vivan los bigotes!
¡Vivan las camisas!
CHICANO #2: Sure, camisas! But is that all you're going to
wear when you go to the mountains? Che Guevara said an
army should take care of its feet. What about your feet, man?
You got gabacho shoes on! I'm a 100% Chicano myself,
because I got soul, baby! I'm a righteous Chicano! Some-

body says viva la raza, I say right on, baby! Somebody says viva la causa, I'm hep, brother. That's how come I say you're fulla shit. Sure we need camisas, but you forgot to mention huaraches! ¡Vivan los bigotes! ¡Vivan las camisas! ¡Vivan los huaraches!

CHICANO #1: Bullshit, you're misleading the people! You're too . . .

CHICANO #2: Too militant? Simon, I'm militant. I'm so militant I scare myself.

CHICANO #1: With that pig face, I believe it.

CHICANO #2: What about you, cara de culo?

CHICANO #1: ¡Puto!

CHICANO #2: ¡Cabrón! (*They pull out cuetes and shoot each other. They fall dead.* GABACHO *comes to the microphone.*)

GABACHO: Ladies and gentlemen, I believe the lecture is concluded. (*Looks down.*) I feel so guilty. (*Laughs.*) Guilty. (*Exits laughing uproariously.*)

Huelguistas

1970

Characters

Campesino Mexicano
Campesino Filipino
Campesino Tejano
Campesina Casada
Campesina Viejita
Campesino Coyote
Ranchero

Enter campesinos huelguistas with picket signs; they are, in order of appearance: CAMPESINO TEJANO, CAMPE- SINO FILIPINO, CAPESINA CASADA, CAMPESINA VIEJITA, CAMPESINO MEXICANO.

CAMPESINOS: (*Singing.*) De colores
de colores se visten los hijos
de ricos rancheros
de colores
de colores son los campesinos
allá en los labores. (*They freeze.*)
CAMPESINO MEXICANO: ¡Quihubo pues, raza! Nosotros somos los huelguistas de César Chávez. ¿No nos conocen? Huy, pues... hasta México ha llegado la noticia muy alegre

que Delano es diferente.

CAMPESINOS: (*Singing.*) Hasta México ha llegado la noticia muy alegre que Delano es diferente! (RANCHERO *enters.*)

RANCHERO: All right, what the hell's the racket out here?

CAMPESINO TEJANO: ¿Pos qué chavo? ¡Huelga, huelga, huelga!

CAMPESINA CASADA: ¡Queremos justicia!

CAMPESINA VIEJITA: ¡Y escusados en los files!

CAMPESINO FILIPINO: ¡Vacaciones con pago!

CAMPESINO TEJANO: ¡Y un contrato de unión!

CAMPESINO MEXICANO: Pues el pueblo ya está en contra, los rancheros engreídos que acaban con la gente.

CAMPESINA CASADA: Nos dicen los patroncitos que el trabajo siempre se hace con bastantes esquiroles.

CAMPESINO COYOTE: You call me, patrón?

RANCHERO: That's right, Coyote! You're supposed to be such a hot labor contractor. Earn the money I pay you!

CAMPESINO TEJANO: Y mandan enganchadores pa' engañar trabajadores que se venden por frijoles.

CAMPESINO COYOTE: ¡Andale pues, raza! ¿Quiénes de ustedes quieren un jalecito?

CAMPESINO MEXICANO: Pero hombres de la raza se fajan y no se rajan.

CAMPESINA VIEJITA: Mientras la uva se hace pasa.

CAMPESINOS: (*Angrily at* COYOTE.) ¡Viva la revolución! ¡Viva nuestra asociación! ¡Viva huelga en general!

CAMPESINO COYOTE: Ya pues, ya. No me muerdan!

CAMPESINO MEXICANO: Ya saben los contratistas que ni caro ni barato comprarán nuestros hermanos.

CAMPESINO COYOTE: Yo sí soy vendido hasta las cachas.

CAMPESINA CASADA: ¡Pero como es bien sabido que pa' mantener familias más sueldos necesitamos!

CAMPESINOS: (*To* COYOTE *and* RANCHERO.) ¡Necesitamos más sueldos! ¡Un contrato de unión!

¡Mejores condiciones de trabajo! ¡Un escusado en el fil!
(COYOTE *and* RANCHERO *run off.*)
CAMPESINO TEJANO: Ya está bueno, compañeros como dice
    César Chávez "Esta huelga ganaremos!"
CAMPESINOS: (*Chant.*) ¡Abajo los contratistas!
    ¡Arriba nuestros huelguistas!
    ¡Que se acabe el esquirol!

(*Singing.*) ¡Viva la huelga en el fil
    viva la causa en la historia
    la raza llena de gloria
    la victoria va cumplir!

Vietnam Campesino

1970

First Performance: At Guadalupe Church in Delano during the annual Thanksgiving gathering of huelguistas and UFWOC supporters.

Characters:

Butt Anglo
General Defense
Little Butt
Don Coyote
Campesino Father
Campesino Mother
Campesino Son
Dolores Huelga
El Draft
Vietnamese Man
Vietnamese Woman
Pickets

The military-agricultural complex. Enter BUTT ANGLO, *chomping on a cigar.*

BUTT: (*To audience.*) Have you seen General Defense? He's from the Pentagon. He just got back from Vietnam. (*Enter anti-war pickets, carrying signs, chanting in unison.*)

PICKETS: Vietnam! Vietnam! Stop the war in Vietnam! (*They repeat chant. Wave picket signs and American flag at* BUTT ANGLO.)

BUTT: Wait a minute, wait a minute! (*Pickets quiet down.*) Why are you yelling at me about the war in Vietnam? I'm just a poor grower.

PICKET: How many acres do you have?

BUTT: Fifty. (*Aside.*) Thousand.

PICKET: How much did you receive in federal subsidies?

BUTT: Peanuts. Only ten dollars more than last year.

PICKET: How much was it last year?

BUTT: Ten dollars less. (*Aside.*) Give or take a couple of million.

PICKET: What are you doing to control pesticides?

BUTT: Pesticides? None of your business! What is this, why all the questions? What do my pesticides have to do with war?

PICKET: Everything!

BUTT: Since when?

PICKET: Since the Grape Strike.

BUTT: You goddamn commie, gimme that flag! (*He grabs the American flag from one of the pickets and swings at them. They disperse, and he chases them out, shouting.*) Student radicals, agitators, dope fiends! (*Turns to audience.*) How do you like that? Anti-war pickets against me, a simple dirt farmer. What this country needs is more law and order. It's not that I'm not used to pickets. I am, but pickets of a different kind. The kind that agitate farmworkers, that boycott grapes, that shout . . . Huelga!

PICKETS: (*Backstage.*) ¡Huelga! ¡Huelga! ¡Huelga! (GENERAL DEFENSE *enters, pursued by a different group of pickets. They are farmworkers and carry UFWOC flags, signs, buttons, etc.* BUTT ANGLO *hides.*)

GENERAL: Wait a minute, wait a minute! Why are you yelling at me about that farm labor strike? I'm a general.

PICKET: How many Chicanos are dying in Vietnam?

GENERAL: Enough. But there's room for you.

PICKET: How many scab grapes did the Pentagon buy from Delano?

GENERAL: Not enough. Wanna buy some?

PICKET: ¿Por qué han muerto tantos mexicanos en esta guerra?

GENERAL: Oh, now hold on there. That is enough! Don't come to me speaking that foreign crap. Who do you think I am?

PICKET: Eres asesino. Murderer! Pig!

GENERAL: (*Pulls out gun and fires at pickets, who disperse and exit.*) Same to you! Greasers, chilichokers, tacobenders! (*To audience.*) How do you like that? Farm labor pickets against me, a professional soldier! The whole country's going nuts. What we need around here is more law and order. (*He turns toward* BUTT ANGLO, *and they spot each other.*)

BUTT: Aren't you . . .?

GENERAL: You must be . . .?

BUTT: And you're . . .?

GENERAL: Butt Anglo!

BUTT: General Defense! (*They shake hands.*)

GENERAL: How are you, General?

BUTT: Just fine, Butt. (*They stop.*)

GENERAL: You're Butt.

BUTT: And you're the General.

GENERAL: That's it. (*They shake hands again.*) How you been, Butt? Why, I haven't seen you since the old Delano Grape Strike. Heard you lost that one. (*Elbows* BUTT *in the ribs, laughs.*)

BUTT: (*Weak laugh.*) Yeah. And I haven't seen you since Cambodia. (*Elbows* GENERAL *in the ribs.*) Heard you lost that one. (*He laughs, then stops abruptly. He and the* GENERAL *look at each other.*)

BOTH: (*Step forward arm in arm.*) We'd better get together on this!

GENERAL: Listen, Butt, I understand you've got a strike in the lettuce fields, right? Well, your troubles are over, you ole Butt. Your government in cooperation with the Dow Chemical Corporation has just created a new lettuce picker.

BUTT: (*Enthusiastic.*) Lettuce picker?

GENERAL: All for you.

BUTT: What's it look like?

GENERAL: Like a Mexican about three feet tall, with arms four feet long. Runs on diesel.

BUTT: Diesel?

GENERAL: Yep. He's a greaser. (*They both laugh.*)

BUTT: (*In good spirits.*) Sounds good. But since you're trying to help me, General, I want to help you. You know all that trouble you've been having recruiting Chicanos for Vietnam, Cambodia and Laos?

GENERAL: What trouble? Mexicans are pouring into the army. We just give 'em a pretty little uniform, a few pesos, a blessing from mamacita, and wham-o, they're on the frontlines. Those boys are just dying to show their machismo.

BUTT: Okay, okay, but you still need a Mexican-American leader. One who will unite all the Mexicans, instill them with a fighting spirit, send them marching down the road to freedom, have them willing to fight and die for the American ideals.

GENERAL: (*During the above he has been asking questions.*) Who? Trini Lopez? Herb Alpert? Ricardo Montalban? Jim Plunkitt? Who is it?

BUTT: Cesar Chavez.

GENERAL: It's a deal. (*Extends hand to conclude deal. Stops.*) Cesar Chavez! You trying to be funny? We don't need his type in the Army.

BUTT: Do you think we need him in Salinas?

GENERAL: We'd better figure out some strategy, Butt! (*They start to pace back and forth.*) Well, Anglo, you got any bright ideas?

BUTT: Maybe. Remember what we used to do during the grape strike?

GENERAL: (*Begins to scratch* BUTT'*s back.*) Sure. I used to buy all your scab grapes and ship 'em to Nam...give 'em to the boys.

BUTT: Right! Now how about buying . . .?

GENERAL: Lettuce? (*Stops scratching.*)

BUTT: Nice, fresh, juicy, tender . . .

GENERAL: Can it, pal, we can't use 'em. What's a GI or Marine going to do with lettuce?

BUTT: Make salads?

GENERAL: In the middle of the jungle, in the rice paddies? Up in a chopper? With grapes, we could at least make raisins.

BUTT: Okay, so you can't use my lettuce. That don't stop you from buying it. The government always buys my crops, and some of them I don't even have to plant. What do I care what you do with the lettuce? Eat it, burn it, smoke it.

GENERAL: What did you say? Smoke it! Butt, you're a genius. Smoke it... (*He thinks.*) Sure, it'll work. The boys will smoke anything over there these days. We'll just dry out the leaves, crush them, and cut 'em with the real stuff. How much lettuce you got?

BUTT: Fifty thousand crates. (BUTT *scratches the* GENERAL'*s back.*)

GENERAL: That oughta blow some minds. How much do you want for them?

BUTT: Figuring all expenses, inflation and all, I figure about . . . (*He is reluctant to go too high.*) a quarter of a million dollars.

GENERAL: Quarter of a million dollars! Are you out of your mind? (BUTT *panics, he starts to quote a lower price.*) Take half a million.

BUTT: (GENERAL *starts scratching his back again.*) Half a million? (*He smiles, backing up into the scratch.* GENERAL *scratches higher.*) Higher.

GENERAL: All right, make it three quarters of a million.

BUTT: (*Realizing what's happening.*) Higher, higher!

GENERAL: What the hell, it's taxpayer's money. One million dollars cash!

BUTT: Sold! (*They shake hands.*) It's nice doing business, ain't it?

BOTH: Agri-business.

GENERAL: Well, old friend, I gotta go. See you next time around, okay, buddy?

BUTT: Right. Same time, same subsidy?

GENERAL: Check.

BUTT: Or money order.

GENERAL: I shall return!

BUTT: I'll be itching to see you.

GENERAL: Any time you need me, just give a holler.

BUTT: Will do!

GENERAL: So long.

BUTT: Adiós.

GENERAL: Bye bye.

BUTT: Toodooloo. (*They exit in opposite directions.*)

Pesticides in the field. Backstage sound: the whirr of a toy airplane, created by a single note played on a trumpet. LITTLE BUTT, the grower's son, enters holding up a small model of a crop duster. He circles the stage with the toy airplane, making passes at an imaginary crop, diving down and spraying pesticides from a baby powder container he holds in his free hand. He circles a second time and stops at downstage center.

LITTLE: Hi, I'm Butt Anglo's son, and I'm crop dusting. (*With a high pitched giggle, he begins to fly his airplane for a third round. DON COYOTE, the farm labor contractor, howls backstage and enters, moving swiftly to the edge of the stage.*)

DON COYOTE: (*To audience.*) Quihúbole. I am Don Coyote, el contratista. I work for Butt Anglo and I'm looking for my scabs, uh, my farmworkers. They should be here by now. ¿No buscan jale ustedes? Any of you looking for work? No? Está a toda madre el trabajo aquí, raza. My boss treats his workers good. Especially me. (*He hears* LITTLE BUTT'*s airplane.*) Ay, the patron's son. (*Waves to him.*) Patroncito!

LITTLE: (*To audience.*) Think I'll have a little fun with the spic. Watch this. (*He angles his airplane toward* DON COYOTE.)

DON COYOTE: (*Sees airplane coming at him.*) Patroncito, no! (LITTLE BUTT *sprays* DON COYOTE *and flies offstage laughing.* DON COYOTE *wheezes, coughs, wretches.*) Pesticides! (*He goes blind.*) En la madre, I can't see! I'm blind! ¡Me quedé ciego! ¡Me estoy muriendo! (*Offstage, campesinos call out. Each from a different direction.*)

PADRE: ¿Patrón?

HIJO: ¿'Apá?

MADRE: ¿Hijo?

DON COYOTE: My farmworkers. They'll see me and I won't see them! (*Campesinos repeat their lines several times, steadily sing song until it becomes a song based on those three words: Patrón, 'Apá, Hijo. They enter dancing to the beat. Meanwhile,* DON COYOTE *rubs his eyes and strains to see. Still half blind, he barks a command to the empty air, his back turned to the campesinos. He orders them to get to work.*) ¡Ya corténsela pues! (*Cracks whip.*) Pos ¿qué traen? (*Campesinos look at each other questioningly. They shrug their shoulders. El* HIJO *starts sniffing the air suspiciously.*)

HIJO: (*Sniffs.*) Fuchi.

MADRE: (*Sniffs.*) Fuchi.

PADRE: (*Sniffs.*) Fuchi. (*He smells his underarms, then steps forward, lifts* DON COYOTE'*s tail and sniffs.*) Fuchi!

PADRE: Cómo jiede.

HIJO: ¡A veneno!

MADRE: Cómo apesta.

HIJO: ¡A pesticides!

DON COYOTE: (*His back turned, trying to locate them, still blind.*) Pesticides? It's been thirty days since they last sprayed this field.

HIJO: Then how come you can't see? (*To his father.*) Está ciego.

PADRE: ¿Está ciego, patrón?

HIJO: Sure, he's blind as a bat. (PADRE *holds huelga flag in front of* DON COYOTE's *eyes.*)

DON COYOTE: I show you who's blind. ¡A jalar! (*He starts cracking whip, blindly. Campesinos back away from him easily.* BUTT ANGLO *enters.* DON COYOTE *grabs him, thinking he is one of the campesinos. The real campesinos all gather a distance away.*) ¡Ajá! Ahora si, now you are going to work. (*He kicks him.*) Vamos, into the field!

BUTT: Heh!

DON COYOTE: Shut up! (*Kicks him again.*)

BUTT: Just a minute!

DON COYOTE: Who's blind now, eh?

BUTT: Coyote!

DON COYOTE: You hear that? That's my patrón. He's coming. Get to work. (*Kicks him again.*)

BUTT: (*Standing up.*) Don Coyote!

DON COYOTE: (*Stops.*) Oh, oh! (*He feels* BUTT ANGLO's *face, his nose, etc.*) Patroncito!

BUTT: (*Enraged.*) What the hell you doing, Coyote?

DON COYOTE: Ay, patrón, forgive me. I didn't know it was you. I . . . I'm blind, boss!

BUTT: Blind?

HIJO: (*To parents.*) ¿No les dije? (*To* BUTT.) It was the pesticides.

BUTT: Who are you?

HIJO: I work for you.

BUTT: Then, why aren't your working? Is this the best you could do, Coyote?

DON COYOTE: Nobody wants to scab, patrón.

BUTT: Shut up!

HIJO: It smells like pesticides here. ¿Verdad?

PADRE: Sí, es cierto.

MADRE: Dile, m'ijo.

BUTT: Pesticides? Why, that's ridiculous. (*Takes a deep breath, chokes.*) That's just a little country smog. Right, Coyote? (DON COYOTE *faints.*) Coyote! (*To farmworkers.*) Stay where you are! (*He picks up* COYOTE*'s head, a couple of short slaps.*) What are you trying to do? Lose my workers?

DON COYOTE: (*Out of his head, singing.*) Viva la huelga en el fil . . .

BUTT: He's out of his head. (*Shakes him.*) Come on, Coyote, snap out of it!

DON COYOTE: (*Comes to.*) I'm sorry, patrón. Your son . . . (*Campesinos move in close.*) Your son . . .

BUTT: (*To campesino.*) Get back! (*To* COYOTE.) What about my son?

DON COYOTE: He was crop dusting.

BUTT: (*Drops him.*) Is that all? Why I thought it was something serious. (*To campesinos.*) Nothing to worry about, amigos. Just a few chlorinated hydrocarbons, mixed in with some organo phosphates. Sounds like a new breakfast food, don't it? Sure it does. Might even go good with your frijoles, mix it in like chile powder. It's harmless.

HIJO: If it's harmless, how come he's blind?

BUTT: He's not blind. Ain't that right, Coyote? (*Reaches for his wallet, pulls out money.*) Look here, can you see this ten dollar bill?

DON COYOTE: No, señor.

BUTT: How about this twenty?

DON COYOTE: Just barely.

BUTT: And this fifty?

DON COYOTE: It's more clearer.

BUTT: This ought to clear it up good. A one hundred dollar bill!

DON COYOTE: Patroncito, I can see again! (*He grabs the money.*)

BUTT: See what I told you? Harmless. And as an added bonus, why don't you go sit in your air-conditioned pick-up for a while? I'll get your people to work.

DON COYOTE: (*Overcome with emotion.*) Ay, patroncito, you're so good!

BUTT: Heh!

DON COYOTE: (*Goes out howling.*) Aaaarrrrooooo! (*Exit.*)

BUTT: (*Chuckling to himself.*) Loves his patrón that Coyote. (*To campesinos.*) Get to work! And make sure you pick lots of lettuce. I just sold a big order to the Department of Defense this morning.

HIJO: Chale, yo no trabajo. (*Sits.*)

PADRE: Ni yo. (*Sits.*)

MADRE: Ni yo tampoco. (*Sits.*)

BUTT: What's going on here?

CAMPESINOS: (*Together.*) ¡Huelga!

BUTT: Huelga? You can't go on strike. You're my scabs! Get up! (*Backstage sound.* LITTLE BUTT's *airplane is heard approaching.*)

BUTT: Sounds like my son. Heh, that gives me an idea. (*Enter* LITTLE BUTT *with toy crop duster and powder can.*)

LITTLE: Hi, Pa, I'm crop dusting.

BUTT: Go to it, son, give 'em hell. (*Aside.*) That'll fix their huelga. (LITTLE BUTT *starts a second run. Enter* DOLORES HUELGA *with a UFWOC flag.*)

DOLORES: Hey! What do you think you're doing?

BUTT: What's it to you? This is my land. Who are you?

DOLORES: ¡Yo soy Dolores Huelga! (*Campesinos cheer "Viva la Huelga", etc.*)

BUTT: (*To campesinos.*) Shut up!

DOLORES: (*Steps in between* BUTT *and* CAMPESINOS.) Shut up yourself! You're spraying pesticides while the workers are still in the fields.

BUTT: That's a damn lie! (LITTLE BUTT *hides airplane behind his back.*)

DOLORES: You're also poisoning the lettuce.

BUTT: So what? It's my lettuce. Now, get of my private property.

DOLORES: (*She backs him up.*) We're going to boycott you, Butt Anglo.

BUTT: (*He forces her to walk back.*) Your boycott doesn't work. I just sold all of my lettuce to a good friend.

DOLORES: Then we're going to launch a campaign against your pesticides.

BUTT: Oh yeah?

DOLORES: Yeah! ¡Huelga, huelga, huelga! (*Pushes* BUTT ANGLO *back until he falls offstage or onto floor.*)" ¡Qué viva la huelga!

CAMPESINOS: ¡Qué viva! (DOLORES HUELGA *exits.*)

LITTLE: I'll get her, Pa. (*He starts to follow* DOLORES HUELGA, *but he spots someone else backstage and freezes.*)

The Farmworker and the draft.

LITTLE: (*Running back in.*) He's coming!

BUTT: (*Getting to his feet.*) Who?

LITTLE: It's him!

BUTT: Him who? (*Suddenly alarmed.*) César Chávez?

LITTLE: No, it's . . . (*Enter a tall figure with a death mask and an American flag for a shroud.*) the draft! (*Sudden pandemonium. El* HIJO *hides behind his farmworker parents and* LITTLE BUTT *hides under his father, between his legs.*)

HIJO: (*Trying to hide.*) ¡En la madre, el draft! 'Amá, 'Apá, díganle que no estoy aquí. Que me fui para México. (*The* DRAFT *surveys the situation coldly, then suddenly points at the young farmworker.*)

PADRE: No está aquí. Se fue pa' México. He go away. (*The* DRAFT *stomps his foot, and points at the young farmworker again.*)

HIJO: (*To audience.*) Míralo, míralo. ¿Qué me cree, pendejo? (*He flips the* DRAFT *a bird.*) ¡Toma! (*To audience.*) Chale con el draft, raza. (*The* DRAFT *stomps his foot and points again.*) You want some more, eh? ¡Pos toma! (*Flips him the bird again. The* DRAFT *reaches behind him and pulls out an imaginary fishing rod. He pantomimes the motions of swinging it and hooking the young campesino.*) ¡No, no, ayúdenme! ¡'Amá, 'Apá, no quiero ir! I don't want to go! (*The* DRAFT *reels him in on his tip toes and throws him offstage.*)

LITTLE: Whew! I thought he was going to get me. (*Looks out at audience.*) Wonder who he's gonna get next? (*Peeks out between* BUTT'*s legs.* DRAFT *goes for* LITTLE, *grabbing between* BUTT'*s legs.*) BUTT: General Defense! (GENERAL DEFENSE *enters immediately and steps between the* DRAFT *and* BUTT.)

GENERAL: Yes, what seems to be the trouble here?

BUTT: He's trying to take my boy.

GENERAL: (*Angrily.*) What's the matter with you, Draft? Haven't I told you to stick to the minorities? Go draft some Mexicans, some Indians, some Blacks, some Asians, some Puerto Ricans. (DRAFT *stands at attention, saluting.*) Now, get out of here. (DRAFT *gestures helplessly, trying to explain.*) I said get! (*The* DRAFT *exits.*) Anglo, you should get your Little Butt in school.

BUTT: I know. That's why I just enrolled him at Fresno State College.

LITTLE: Oh boy! Do they have airplanes there, Pa?

BUTT: They got airplanes, they got girls, they got everything, son. You just go git some!

LITTLE: Oh boy! I'm gonna git me some. (*He exits.*)

GENERAL: That's a fine future leader you got there, Butt.

BUTT: (*Shakes his hand.*) Once again I'm indebted to you, General.

GENERAL: That's what we're here for, pal. To provide for the general defense, promote the general welfare . . .

BUTT: Welfare!

GENERAL: I mean, subsidy. To promote the federal subsidies, and to secure the blessings of liberty . . .

BUTT: In that case, I do have one small problem I'd like to discuss with you.

GENERAL: What is it?

BUTT: Well, I realize you've bought all my lettuce and I appreciate it, but, ahh . . .

GENERAL: Come on, Butt, spit it out.

BUTT: In addition to this huelga-boycott nonsense. (*He spots campesinos straining to hear.*) Over here. (*He and the* GENERAL *move to one side.*) They've also launched a campaign against pesticides.

GENERAL: So what?

BUTT: So, they want to turn the American public against me!

GENERAL: Just because of pesticides? Nobody's been able to do it with germicides, or napalm, or even genocide. And after ten years in Vietnam, I oughta know, pal. It's all matter of public relations. For instance, who's been giving you all this trouble?

BUTT: That's just the point. They're farmwokers, campesinos, poor people.

GENERAL: Communists, right? Well, let me show you what we got over here in Vietnam.

Vietnam campesinos. Two Vietnamese peasants enter quietly and sit down at stage left. The campesinos MADRE *and* PADRE *are sitting quietly at stage right.* BUTT ANGLO *and the* GENERAL *move between them for the rest of the acto.*

GENERAL: (*Points at Vietnamese.*) Farmworkers just like them farmworkers. (*Points at campesinos, then back at Vietnamese.*) Campesinos just like them campesinos. (*Points again.*) Poor people just like them poor people. (*Points again.*) And we've been killing them for ten years.

BUTT: Ten years?

GENERAL: It's been open season over there.

BUTT: A regular gook shot.

GENERAL: Exactly . . . gooks! They aren't people, they're gooks. (*Goes over to campesinos.*) And these are greasers, spics, chili-ass taco benders. They deserve to die.

BUTT: Hold on, General. I don't think the public will go for that.

GENERAL: Of course they won't, at first. You gotta build up to it. And the first step is to attack the leadership. Now, over in Vietnam, we got a thing called the National Liberation Front. (*Vietnamese male takes out NLF flag and waves it.*) Hey! (*He puts flag away.*) But do you think we call it that? Hell no, we give it a good ugly sounding name. A name you want to kill, you want to destroy! Like Cong. Viet Cong! (*Menaces Veitnamese.*) Dirty Asiatic bastards, I could kill 'em right now.

BUTT: Go ahead.

GENERAL: What's the name of the union?

BUTT: The United Farm Workers Organization Committee. (*Campesino waves huelga flag.*) Heh! (*He puts flag away.*)

GENERAL: Naw, that's too clean, too decent. Who's the leadership?

BUTT: César Chávez and Larry Itliong.

GENERAL: (*A sudden inspiration.*) The Chávez-Itliong gang! The Chong!

BUTT: Chong?

GENERAL: The Communist Mexican Chong!

BUTT: Dirty, stinking Mexican Chong! (*Turns to campesinos.*)

GENERAL: That's the idea.

BUTT: Goddamn Chong! (*Goes over to campesinos.*)

GENERAL: Keep it up.

BUTT: Communist Chong! (*Menaces campesinos.*)

GENERAL: One more time.

BUTT: Dirty, stinking, Communist Mexican Chong! I could kill 'em.

GENERAL: Beautiful! Only don't kill 'em yet. First you gotta have some allies.

BUTT: What kind of allies.

GENERAL: The good guys. A phoney political front fighting the reds.

BUTT: Like the Saigon government?

GENERAL: (*Frowns.*) Like a phoney union.

BUTT: Phoney union? We've already tried that. It doesn't work. Watch this. (*Calls out.*) Don Coyote!

DON COYOTE: (*Backstage howl.*) Aaaarrooo. (*Enters.*) You call me, patrón?

BUTT: Get them to join our union.

DON COYOTE: But, boss, they don't want to. We already tried to . . .

BUTT: Shut up and do your stuff!

DON COYOTE: Yes, boss. (*Goes over to campesinos.*) Quihúbole, ¿cómo les va de jale?

PADRE: Pos aquí nomás nos están envenenando.

DON COYOTE: Pos, ¿quién se los manda?

PADRE: ¿Qué?

DON COYOTE: Les traigo unos consejos. Miren, no se junten con César Chávez. Es comunista. ¡Colorado hasta las cachas! Júntense con una unión responsable. La unión de mi patrón. Miren. (*He pulls out sign with initals A.W.F.W.A.*) AWFWA!

CAMPESINOS: ¿Qué es eso?

DON COYOTE: The Agricultural Workers Freedom to Work Association.

CAMPESINOS: ¿Qué?

DON COYOTE: AWFWA.

CAMPESINOS: ¿Qué?

DON COYOTE: AWFWA.

CAMPESINOS: ¿Qué?

CON COYOTE: AWWWFWAAA!

PADRE: Salud.

DON COYOTE: Gracias. (*Turns, stops.*) Pos, mira qué jijos . . . (*Pause. Regains composure.*) No se asusten, ahorita vuelvo. (*DON COYOTE joins BUTT ANGLO and the GENERAL in a huddle. They mumble and scheme inaudibly, then stop suddenly. DON COYOTE turns around with a new sign with initals M.A.C.*)

DON COYOTE: Mac! El Big Mac!

PADRE: ¿Qué es eso?

DON COYOTE: Mothers Against Chávez.

MADRE: ¿Qué?

DON COYOTE: ¡Que Madres en contra de Chávez!

PADRE: ¡La tuya!

DON COYOTE: ¿La mía? (*DON COYOTE runs back to BUTT and the GENERAL, and they form a new huddle. Incomprehensible mumbling and scheming again. Then they all snap to attention, in a line, their backs to the audience.*

GENERAL: Achtung! (*The GENERAL, BUTT ANGLO and DON COYOTE turn around in close formation, stomping vigorously, then they march forward, toward campesinos, in a Nazi goose step. They come to stop directly in front of farmworkers. COYOTE carries a new sign, reading T.E.A.M.S.T.E.R.S.*

DON COYOTE: Teamsters! Jabol?

GENERAL: Ya?

GROWER: Yes?

CAMPESINOS: (*Pause. They look at each other.*) No!

DON COYOTE: It's no use, boss. They're either too stupid, or they're getting smart.

BUTT: You're the one that's too stupid. Get out of here! (*DON COYOTE exits with a howl.*) See what I mean, General?

GENERAL: No, I don't see! If you want them to be Teamsters, you just tell them they're Teamsters! Don't pussyfoot around, Butt! We're fighting a war, boy. Now I want you to watch carefully what we've done over here in Vietnam. Introducing the democratic, pro-U.S. South Vietnamese President, Ding Dong Diem! (*Enter* DON COYOTE *dressed as* PRESIDENT DIEM. *He wears a baseball hat with silver decorations, dark glasses, a colorful scarf and on orange U.S. Navy aviator's safety jacket. Shaking his hand.*) President Ding, how's your dong?

PRESIDENT: Ding, ding.

GENERAL: Do your stuff. (*The* PRESIDENT *walks over to Vietnamese. He begins to repeat the exact words the* GENERAL *whispers to him.*)

PRESIDENT: My fellow Vietnamese.

GENERAL: I am.

PRESIDENT: I am.

GENERAL: Your democratic.

PRESIDENT: Your democratic.

GENERAL: South Vietnamese.

PRESIDENT: South Vietnamese.

GENERAL: President.

PRESIDENT: President.

GENERAL: Diem!

PRESIDENT: Diem! (*He bends forward at the waist, holding up a sign reading "President Diem."*)

VIETNAMESE: (*Together, thumbs down.*) Chingao!

GENERAL: There's more.

PRESIDENT: There's more.

GENERAL: President Hu Nos Hu.

PRESIDENT: Hu Nos Hu! (*Bends forward, sign reads "Hu Nos Hu."*)

VIETNAMESE: Chingao!

GENERAL: There's more. President Dan Ky Ho Ti.

PRESIDENT: Dan Ky Ho Ti! (*Bends forward, sign reads "Don Coyote."*)

VIETNAMESE: Chingao!

GENERAL: Chingao, hell! This one you're gonna have to

accept! Here you are, Mr. President! (*Gives him a gun.*)

PRESIDENT: (*Shoots one of the Vietnamese, holds gun against his head and gives speech.*) We South Vietnamese are a peace-loving people, and we ask you Americans to keep sending your troops to South Vietnam for as long as we need them. Thank you. How was that, General? (*Hands back gun.*)

GENERAL: Just fine, Mr. President. Here you are. (*Gives him wad of bills.*) Go buy yourself a case of Cokes. (GENERAL *holds out hand at the same time the* PRESIDENT *salutes and the* PRESIDENT *holds out hand.*) Sorry. (*The* GENERAL *and* PRESIDENT *keep shaking and saluting out of order, going faster each time trying to catch up. The* GENERAL *finally gives up.*) Get out of here! (*The South Vietnamese president exits. Campesinos have been watching intently.*)

PADRE: (*To his wife.*) Oye, vieja, esas gentes son iguales que nosotros.

MADRE: ¿Verdad que sí? Y a ellos también les dicen comunistas.

PADRE: Pero nomás son pobres campesinos. (*To Vietanmese.*) ¡Oye, Vietnam! (*Vietnamese turn toward campesinos.* PADRE *and* MADRE *give them the peace sign.*)

BUTT: (*Going over to campesinos.*) What the hell's going on over here? You see, General, it didn't work! They're worse than ever.

GENERAL: They are, huh? Then it's time to escalate the war a bit.

BUTT: What do we do?

GENERAL: We'll burn down their houses!

BUTT: My labor camp?

GENERAL: Kill their women and children!

BUTT: My pickers!

GENERAL: You can worry about your pickers later. Right now we want to teach them a lesson. And for this we need soldiers, the army. (*Barks a command.*) U.S. Infantry, up front!

The Chicano at War. A trumpet plays reveille. El HIJO, *The young campesino, now re-enters dressed as an infantryman in battle gear. He salutes the* GENERAL.)

HIJO: Yes, sir!

GENERAL: I want you to burn the house of these farmworkers, boy.

HIJO: Yes, sir! (*The soldier moves toward the campesinos, who hold up a paper cut out of a small labor camp shack. They wave at him.*)

CAMPESINOS: Hello, hijo.

HIJO: (*Turns back to* GENERAL.) Heh, I can't burn my parent's home.

GENERAL: Not those farmworkers, stupid. (*Points at Vietnamese.*) These farmworkers.

HIJO: Oh, yes, sir. (*He burns the Vietnamese shack — a paper cut out.*)

GENERAL: Okay, stomp it out.

HIJO: (*Stomps out fire.*) How's that, sir?

GENERAL: Just fine, soldier. (*He salutes and everything goes into slow motion. His voice, his salute, the soldier's salute, etc.*) Dismissssseeddd. (*The soldier finishes the slow motion salute and turns to exit. One of the Vietnamese spins around with a rifle and shoots him.*)

HIJO: Ay! (*He pitches forward, offstage, dying.*)

MADRE: (*Crying out.*) ¡M'ijito! (*All motion goes back to normal pace. The* MADRE *weeps in her husband's arms.*)

GENERAL: I'll be goddamn, they got him.

BUTT: Now what?

GENERAL: (*Points to campesinos.*) Now we give them a medal, of course. Okay, señora, on your feet. (*Campesinos rise in grief and shock. Taps play in background.*) In recognition of your son's valorous service to his country, I hereby award you the . . . (*Reaches in his pocket.*) Purple Heart. (*To* PADRE.) Well, amigo, how do you feel now?

Still love them gooks over there?

PADRE: (*To Vietnamese.*) ¡Desgraciados comunistas! ¡Mataron a m'ijo!

GENERAL: You're right, pop. They killed your boy. Shot him in the back.

PADRE: ¡Cobardes! (*He tries to rush Vietnamese.*)

GENERAL: Heh, heh, hold it. You're too old to go over there and fight. (*Restrains him.*)

PADRE: ¡Malvados! ¡Animales! (*He struggles to get free.*)

GENERAL: Come on, now! Let the young do the fighting. (PADRE *calms down.*) How about it, papa, you got anymore young Chicanos at home?

MADRE: (*To* GENERAL.) No! (*She embraces* PADRE *and they sit down.*)

GENERAL: Just asking. Thought you might like another crack at 'em. Okay, Butt, having pacified the countryside, so to speak, we're now ready for the final step.

BUTT: Which is?

GENERAL: Which is the use of a new secret weapon, developed at the Dow Chemical laboratories! (*A trumpet fanfare. Two heads of lettuce appear at opposite ends of stage.* BUTT *retrieves one, and the* GENERAL *the other.*)

BUTT: (*Picking up lettuce.*) This is it?

GENERAL: It sure is.

BUTT: What do you mean, secret weapon? This looks like lettuce. It feels like lettuce. It even . . . (*Starts to bite lettuce.*)

GENERAL: Stop! Don't even breathe on it, Butt. There's enough DDT on that lettuce to kill five men.

BUTT: DDT?

GENERAL: You heard me.

BUTT: (*Begins to grin.*) Pesticides.

GENERAL: Don't tell anybody. And to deliver these bombs, we need air power. The Strategic Air Command. (BUTT *and the* GENERAL *face each other and begin to sing "Off we go, into the wild blue yonder!"* LITTLE BUTT, *in jet pilot's gear, enters between them.* LITTLE: Hi, paw.

BUTT: Son! What are you doing here?

GENERAL: I convinced him to join the AFROTC at Fresno State College. He's going to be an officer and a gentlemen. He might even go to the moon someday. Are you ready, officer?

LITTLE: Yessir!

GENERAL: Put on your helmet. (LITTLE BUTT *puts on helmet.*) Load wing tanks! (LITTLE BUTT *stretches out his arms like wings. Drumroll. The* GENERAL *and* BUTT ANGLO *place the two lettuces in his hands. Then retrieving a black cloth each from backstage, they lay these over* LITTLE BUTT'*s arms. He looks like a deadly bird.*)

BUTT: Loaded.

GENERAL: Loaded. Contact.

BUTT: Contact.

GENERAL: Rev up motors. (BUTT *and the* GENERAL *swing their arms around slowly.* LITTLE BUTT *begins to swing back and forth on his feet, as if getting ready for take off. On the third swing, the* GENERAL *and* BUTT ANGLO *point forward.* LITTLE BUTT *takes off.*) Take off! (*With a scream of engines, backstage noises* LITTLE BUTT *flies into position and zeroes in for the kill. He drops a lettuce bomb on the male campesino then on the Vietnamese. He swings around and comes back for the women, covering their faces with a black cloth each. Depending on the circumstances, slides of Vietnam, farm labor, crop dusting, dead bodies, etc. may be shown during this sequence. The women cough and choke underneath the black cloths. All die.*)

BUTT: My boy did that.

GENERAL: Good work, officer. Attention! Left face. (LITTLE BUTT *turns right.*)

BUTT: The other way, stupid. (LITTLE BUTT *turns left.*)

GENERAL: In recognition of your valorous service to your country in the skies of South Vietnam, North Vietnam, Cambodia and Laos, I hereby award you the Distinguished Flying Cross, two months paid vacation in Hawaii and a new refrigerator. Dismissed. (LITTLE BUTT *salutes and exits.*) Well, Butt, there you are: mission accomplished. You spray pesticiedes, and I bomb Vietnam.

BUTT: Yeah, but I still say the American public will never buy it.

GENERAL: Never buy it? Hell, who do you think has bought it for the last ten years. You get the Whites to pay for it, and the Chicanos, the Blacks, Indians and Orientals to fight it. (*Goes over to Vietnamese.*) So what if we've killed the people? We've saved the country from Communism.

BUTT: Saved it from Communism.

GENERAL: (*Goes over to farmworkers.*) So what if you've poisoned the farmworkers? You've saved the crop from Communism.

BUTT: Saved the crop from . . . (*Pause. Realizes.*) Heh, wait a minute. If you poison the workers, you also poison the crop. And if you poison the crop, who's going to buy it? (*Moves over to Vietnamese.*) And over here, if you kill the people, what are you saving? What are you doing over there anyway?

GENERAL: Butt, you ask me what we're doing in Vietnam? You know damn well what we're doing in Vietnam! We're over there. (*Angered.*) We're over there . . .

BUTT: Fighting Communism?

GENERAL: Buying your scab lettuce, pal?

BUTT: It all comes back to me now.

GENERAL: Shall we go sign a bill of sale?

BUTT: Con mucho gusto. (GENERAL *defense and* BUTT ANGLO *exit. Pause. The Chicano soldier re-enters, with blood on his forehead.*)

HIJO: The war in Vietnam continues, asesinando familias inocentes de campesinos. Los Chicanos mueren en la guerra, y los rancheros se hacen ricos, selling their scab products to the Pentagon. The fight is here, Raza! En Aztlán.

VIETNAMESE WOMAN: (*Rises.*) En Aztlán.

MADRE: (*Rises.*) En Aztlán.

VIETNAMESE MAN: (*Rises.*) En Aztlán.

PADRE: (*Rises.*) En Aztlán. (*They all raise their fists in the air, in silence.*)

Soldado Razo

1971

First Performance: April 3, 1971, in Fresno, California, at the Chicano Moratorium on the War in Vietnam.

Characters:

Johnny
La Mamá
El Jefito
Cecilia
La Muerte
El Hermano

MUERTE: (*Enters singing.*) "Me voy de soldado razo, voy ingresar a las filas con los valientes muchachos que dejan madres queridas, que dejan novias llorando, llorando, llorando su despedida." Ajúa! Pos, que a toda madre para mí que hay guerra. Quihubo pues, raza. Yo soy la Muerte. ¿Qué nuevas, no? Bueno, no se escamen porque I didn't come to take anybody away. I came to tell you a story. Simón, the story of the Soldado Razo. Maybe you knew him, eh? He was killed not too long ago in Vietnam. (JOHNNY *enters adjusting his uniform.*) This is Johnny, el Soldado Razo. He's leaving for Vietnam in the morning, but tonight, bueno, tonight he's going to enjoy himself,

¿verdad? Look at his face. Know what he's thinking? He's thinking. (JOHNNY *moves his lips.*) "Ahora sí, I'm a man!" (*La* MAMA *enters.*) This is his jefita. Pobrecita. She's worried about her son, como todas las madres. "Bendito sea Dios," she's thinking. (MAMA *moves mouth.*) Ojalá y no le pase nada a m'ijo." (MAMA *touches* JOHNNY *on the shoulder.*)

JOHNNY: ¿Ya está la cena, jefa?

MAMA: Sí, hijo, ya merito. Pero, ¿por qué te vestiste así? No vas hasta mañana.

JOHNNY: Pos, ya sabe. Va a venir Cecilia y todo.

MAMA: Ay, qué m'ijo. Me traes mil novias, pero nunca te casas.

JOHNNY: Pos, a ver cuando le caigo con un surprise, 'Amá. (*He kisses her forehead. Embraces her.*)

MUERTE: ¡Orale! Qué picture de tenderness, ¿no? Pero watcha la jefita. Listen to what she's thinking. "Ahora sí, m'ijo es hombre. Se mira tan simpático en ese uniforme."

JOHNNY: Bueno, jefita, it's getting late. Al rato vuelvo con Cecilia, ¿eh?

MAMA: Sí, hijo, vuelve pronto. (*He leaves.*) Dios te cuide, corazón de tu madre. (JOHNNY *re-enters and begins to walk.*)

MUERTE: Out in the street, Johnny begins to think about his family, his girl, his barrio, his life.

JOHNNY: Chihuahua, pobre jefita. Mañana va a ser muy duro para ella. También para mí. It was pretty hard when I went to boot camp, ¿pero ahora? Vietnam! 'Ta cabrón, man. The jefito también. I'm not going to be here to help him out. No me estaba haciendo rico en el jale, but it was something. Una alivianada siquiera. El carnalillo no puede trabajar todavía porque está en la escuela. I hope he stays there también. And finishes. A mí nunca me cayó ese jale, but I know the carnalillo digs it. He's smart too. Maybe he'll even go to college. One of us has got to make it in this life. Me, I guess I'll just get married con Cecilia and have a bola de chavalos. I remember when I first saw her at the Rainbow. I couldn't even dance with her porque me había echado mis birrias. The next week was pretty good, though. Desde entonces. How long ago was that? June . . . no, July. Four months. Ahora me quiero ranar con ella. Her parents don't like me, I know. They think I'm a vago. Maybe they'll feel different when I come back from Nam. Simón, el war veteran! Maybe I'll get wounded and come back con un chingatal de medals. I wonder how the vatos around here are going to think about that? Pinche barrio. I've lived here all my life. Now I'm going to Vietnam. I might even get killed. If I do, they'll bring me back here in a box, covered with the flag . . . military funeral like they gave Pete Gómez . . . everybody crying . . . la jefita. What am I thinking, man? ¡Estoy loco! (LA MUERTE *powders* JOHNNY*s face white during next speech.*)

MUERTE: Loco, pero no pendejo, ¿eh? He knew the kind of funeral he wanted and he got it. Military coffin, muchas flores, American flag, mujeres llorando and a trumpet playing taps with a rifle salute at the end. Or was it goodbye? You know what I mean. It was first class all the way. Oh, by the way, no se agüiten con el make-up I'm putting on him, eh? I'm just getting him ready for what's coming. I don't always do things in a hurry, you know. Orale pues, next scene. (JOHNNY *exits.*) Back en la casa, his jefito is just getting home. (EL PAPA *enters.*)

PAPA: ¿Vieja? Ya vine. ¿Ya está la cena? (MAMA *enters.*)

MAMA: Sí, viejo. Espérate nomás que llegue Juan. ¿Qué compraste?

PAPA: Un sixpack de Coors.

MAMA: ¿Cerveza?

PAPA: Pues, ¿por qué no? Mira, si ésta es la última noche de m'ijo, ¿qué?

MAMA: ¿Cómo que última noche? No hables así, hombre.

PAPA: Digo que la última noche en casa, mujer. Tú me comprendes, hip.

MAMA: Andas tomado, ¿verdad?

PAPA: Y si ando, ¿qué te importa? Nomás me eché unas cuantas heladas con mi compadre y es todo. Pos, mira . . . Ahora si parió la burra seca, hombre. M'ijo se va a la guerra y no quieres que tome. ¡Si hay que celebrar, mujer!

MAMA: ¿Celebrar qué?

PAPA: ¡Que m'ijo ya es hombre! Y bien macho. Así es que no me alegues. Traime de cenar.

MAMA: Espérate que venga Juan.

PAPA: ¿Dónde está? ¿No está aquí? ¿Que salió de vago el desgraciado? ¿Juan? ¿Juan?

MAMA: Te digo que se fue a traer a Cecilia, que va a cenar con nosotros. Y por favor no hables tantas cochinadas, hombre. ¿Qué dirá la muchacha si te oye hablar así?

PAPA: ¡Con una jodida, mujer! ¿Pos de quién es esta casa? ¿No soy yo el que paga la renta? ¿El que compra la comida? No me hagas enojar, ¿eh? O te va muy mal. No le hace que ya tengas un hijo soldado.

MAMA: Por favor, viejo. Te lo pido por tu hijo, ¿eh? Cálmate. (*She exits.*)

PAPA: ¿Bah? ¡Cálmate! Nomás así quiere que me calme. ¿Y quién me va a callar? ¿M'ijo el soldado? M'ijo . . .

MUERTE: The jefito's thoughts are racing back a dozen years to a warm afternoon in July. Johnny, eight years old, is running toward him between the vines, shouting, "Apaaaa, ya pizqué veinte tablas, papáaa."

PAPA: Huh. Veinte tablas. Mocoso. (*El* HERMANO *enters.*)

HERMANO: 'Apá, is Johnny here?

MUERTE: This is Johnny's carnalito.

PAPA: Y tú, ¿de dónde vienes?

HERMANO: Allá andaba en Polo's house. Tiene un motor scooter nuevo.

PAPA: Tú nomás te la llevas jugando, ¿no?

HERMANO: Yo no hice nada.

PAPA: No me resongues.

HERMANO: (*Shrugs.*) ¿Ya vamos a cenar?

PAPA: Yo no sé. Ve, pregúntale a tu madre. (HERMANO *exits.*)

MUERTE: Looking at his younger son, the jefito se pone a pensar de él. His thoughts spin around in the usual hopeless cycle of defeat, undercut by more defeat.

PAPA: Ese muchacho ya debe de andar trabajando. Ya tiene sus catorce años cumplidos. Yo no sé porqué la ley los obliga que vayan a la escuela hasta los diez y seis. Al cabo, no va a llegar a ser nada. Mejor que se meta a trabajar conmigo pa' que ayude a la familia.

MUERTE: Simón, se sale de la escuela en three or four years, I take him the way I took Johnny. ¿Qué loco, no, raza? (JOHNNY *returns with* CECILIA.)

JOHNNY: Buenas noches, 'Apá.

PAPA: ¡Hijo! Buenas noches. Ay pos, mira, ¿ya andas de soldado otra vez?

JOHNNY: Traje a Cecilia a cenar con nosotros.

PAPA: Pos, que entre, que entre.

CECILIA: Muchas gracias.

PAPA: Qué bien se mira m'ijo, ¿verdad?

CECILIA: Sí, señor.

PAPA: Pos, sí. Ya se nos va de soldado razo. (*Pause.*) Bueno, vamos a ver . . . uh, hijo, ¿no gustas una cervecita?

JOHNNY: Sí, señor, pero, ¿no hay una silla primero? ¿Para Cecilia?

PAPA: Como no. Sí aquí tenemos de todo. Déjame traer. ¿Vieja? ¡Ya llegó la visita! (*He exits.*)

JOHNNY: How you doing?

CECILIA: Okay. Te quiero.

MUERTE: This, of course, is Johnny's novia. Fine, eh? Too bad he'll never get to marry her. Oh, he proposed tonight y todo and she accepted, but she doesn't know what's ahead. Listen to what she's thinking. (CECILIA *moves her mouth.*) "When we get married I hope Johnny still has his uniform. We'd look so good together. Me in a wedding gown and him like that. Chihuahua, I wish we were getting married tomorrow!"

JOHNNY: ¿Qué estás pensando?

CECILIA: Nothing.

JOHNNY: Come on.

CECILIA: Really.

JOHNNY: Chale, I saw your eyes. Now, come on, dime, qué estabas pensando.

CECILIA: It was nothing.

JOHNNY: Are you scared?

CECILIA: About what?

JOHNNY: My going to Vietnam.

CECILIA: No! I mean . . . yes, in a way, but I wasn't thinking that.

JOHNYY: What was it?

CECILIA: (*Pause.*) I was thinking I wish the boda was tomorrow.

JOHNNY: Really?

CECILIA: Yes.

JOHNNY: ¿Sabes qué? I wish it was too. (*He embraces her.*)

MUERTE: And, of course, now he's thinking too. But it's not what she was thinking. ¡Qué raza! (EL PAPA *and the* HERMANO *enter with four chairs.*)

PAPA: Aquí vienen las sillas. ¿No que no? (*To the* HERMANO.) A ver, tú, ayúdame a mover la mesa, ándale.

JOHNNY: ¿Necesita ayuda, 'Apá?

PAPA: No, hijo, yo y tu hermano la movemos. (*He and the* HERMANO *move imaginary table into place.*) Ahi 'ta. Y dice tu mamá que ya se vayan sentando porque ya está la cena. Hizo tamales, ¡fíjate!

JOHNNY: ¡Tamales!

HERMANO: They're Colonel Sanders, eeehh.

PAPA: ¡Tú cállate el hocico! Mira . . . no le haga caso, Cecilia, a este cabrón. Uh, este huerco siempre anda con sus tonterías. Siéntense.

MAMA: (*Entering with imaginary bowl.*) ¡Aquí vienen los tamales! Cuidado porque la olla está caliente, ¿eh? Oh, Cecilia, buenas noches, hija.

CECILIA: Buenas noches, señora. ¿Le puedo ayudar en algo?

MAMA: No, no, ya está todo listo. Siéntese por favor.

JOHNNY: 'Amá, how come you made tamales? (*La* MUERTE *begins to put more make-up on* JOHNNY'*s face.*)

MAMA: Pos, ya sé como te gustan tanto, hijo.

MUERTE: A thought flashes across Johnny's mind. "Too much, man. I should go to war every day." Over on this side of the table, the carnalillo is thinking. "What's so hot about going to war . . . tamales?"

HERMANO: I like tamales.

PAPA: ¿Quién te dijo que abrieras la boca? ¿Gustas una cerveza, hijo?

JOHNNY: (*Nods.*) Gracias, jefe.

PAPA: ¿Y usted, Cecilia?

CECILIA: (*Surprised.*) No, señor, uh, gracias.

MAMA: Juan, hombre, no seas tan imprudente. Cecilia no tiene la edad pa' tomar. ¿Qué dirán sus padres? Hice Kool-Aid, hija, ahorita traigo el picher. (*She exits.*)

PAPA: ¿Cuántos años tienes, Cecilia?

CECILIA: Diez y ocho.

MUERTE: She lied, of course.

PAPA: Oh, pos, qué caray, ¡si ya eres mujer! Andale, hijo, no dejes que se te escape.

JOHNNY: I'm not.

MAMA: (*Re-entering.*) Aquí está el Kool-Aid y los frijoles.

JOHNNY: 'Amá, I got an announcement to make. ¿Se quiere sentar, por favor?

MAMA: ¿Qué es?

PAPA: (*To* HERMANO.) Dale tu silla a tu mamá.

HERMANO: What about my tamale?

MAMA: Déjalo que cene.

PAPA: (*To* HERMANO.) ¡Quítate!

JOHNNY: Siéntese, 'Amá.

MAMA: ¿Qué es hijo? (*She sits down.*)

MUERTE: Funny little games que juega la gente, ¿no? The mother asks, but she already knows what her son is going to say. So does the father. And even little brother. They are all thinking, "He is going to say, '¡Yo y Cecilia nos vamos a casar!'"

JOHNNY: ¡Yo y Cecilia nos vamos a casar!

MAMA: Ay, m'ijo.

PAPA: ¡No, hombre!

HERMANO: Really?

MAMA: ¿Cuándo, hijo?

JOHNNY: When I get back from Vietnam.

MUERTE: Suddenly a thought is crossing everybody's mind, "¿y si no regresa?" But they shove it aside.

MAMA: ¡Ay, m'ija! (*She hugs* CECILIA.)

PAPA: Felicitaciones, hijo. (*He hugs* JOHNNY.)

MAMA: (*Hugging* JOHNNY.) ¡Hijo de mi alma! (*She cries.*)

JOHNNY: Eh, jefa, wait a minute. Save that for tomorrow. Ya pues, 'Amá.

PAPA: Hija. (*He hugs* CECILIA *properly.*)

HERMANO: Heh, Johnny, why don't I go to Vitnam and you stay here for the wedding? I'm not afraid to die.

MAMA: ¿Por qué dices eso, muchacho?

HERMANO: Se me salió.

PAPA: Ya se te salió mucho, ¿no crees?

HERMANO: I didn't mean it! (HERMANO *exits.*)

JOHNNY: It was an accident, 'Apá.

MAMA: Sí, pues, fue accidente. Por favor, viejito, vamos a cenar en paz, ¿eh? Mañana se va Juan.

MUERTE: The rest of the cena pasa sin ningún problema. They discuss the wedding, the tamales and the weather. Then it's time to go to the party.

PAPA: ¿Qué va a haber party?

JOHNNY: A small dance nomás, allá en la casa del Sapo.

MAMA: ¿A cuál Sapo, hijo?

JOHNNY: Sapo, mi amigo.

PAPA: No te vayas a emborrachar, ¿eh?

JOHNNY: Chale, jefe, va ir la Cecilia conmigo.

PAPA: ¿Ya le pediste permiso a sus padres?

JOHNNY: Sí, señor. She's got to be home by eleven.

PAPA: Está bien. (JUAN *and* CECILIA *rise.*)

CECILIA: Gracias por la cena, señora.

MAMA: Ay, hija, no hay de que.

CECILIA: The tamales were really good.

JOHNNY: Sí, 'Amá, estuvieron a todo dar.

MAMA: ¿Sí, hijo? ¿Te gustaron?

JOHNNY: They were great. (*He hugs her.*) Gracias, ¿eh?

MAMA: ¿Cómo que gracias? Eres m'ijo. Váyanses pues, que se hace tarde.

PAPA: ¿No quieres usar la troquita, hijo?

JOHNNY: No, gracias, 'Apá. Ya traigo el carro de Cecilia.

CECILIA: Not mine. My parents' car. They loaned it to us for the dance.

PAPA: Parece que dejaste buena impresión, ¿eh?

CECILIA: He sure did. They say he's more responsible now that he's in the service.

MUERTE: (*To audience.*) Did you hear that? Listen to her again.

CECILIA: (*Repeats sentence, exactly as before.*) They say he's more responsible now that he's in the service.

MUERTE: ¡Así me gusta!

PAPA: Qué bueno. Entonces, nomás nos queda ir a pedirles la mano de Cecilia, ¿no vieja?

MAMA: Si Dios quiere.

JOHNNY: Buenas noches.

CECILIA: Buenas noches.

PAPA: Buenas noches, hija.

MAMA: Cuidado en el camino, hijos.

JOHNNY: Don't worry, jefa . . . be back later.

CECILIA: Bye! (JOHNNY *and* CECILIA *exit. The* MAMA

stands at the door.)

PAPA: (*Sitting down again.*) Pues sí, viejita, ya se nos hizo hombre el Juanito. Qué pronto se pasan los años, ¿no?

MUERTE: The jefito is thinking about the Korean War. Johnny was born about that time. He wishes he had some advice, some consejos, to pass on to him about the guerra. But he never went to Korea. The draft skipped him and somehow he never got around to enlisting.

MAMA: (MAMA *turns around. Sees la* MUERTE.) ¡Valgame Dios! (*Exit.*)

MUERTE: (*Ducking down.*) Shit! I think she saw me.

PAPA: ¿Qué te pasa? (*The* MAMA *is standing frozen, looking toward the spot where la* MUERTE *was standing.*) Contéstame, pues, ¿qué traes? (*Pause.*) Oyes, pos si no estoy aquí pintado. ¡Háblame!

MAMA: (*Solemnly.*) Acabo de ver a la Muerte.

PAPA: ¿Muerte? Estás loca.

MAMA: Es cierto. ¡Salió Juan ahorita, voltié y allí estaba la Muerte parada sonriéndose! (PAPA *moves away from the spot inadvertantly.*) Ave María Purísima, ¿si acaso le pasa algo a Juan?

PAPA: ¡Ya cállate el hocico! ¿Que no ves que es mala suerte? (*They exit.* MUERTE *re-enters.*)

MUERTE: The next day, Johnny goes to the Greyhound Bus Depot. His mother, his father and his novia go with him to say goodbye. The bus depot is full of soldiers and sailors and old men. Here and there, a wino is passed out on the benches. Then there's the announcements: "The Los Angeles bus is now receiving passengers at gate two for Kingsburg, Tulare, Delano, Bakersfield and Los Angeles, connections Los Angeles for points east and south." (JOHNNY, PAPA, MAMA *and* CECILIA *enter.* CECILIA *clings to* JOHNNY.)

PAPA: Ya hace muchos años que no me he pasiado en el estache.

MAMA: ¿Tienes tu tíquete, hijo?

JOHNNY: Ay no, I got to buy it.

CECILIA: I'll go with you.

PAPA: ¿Traes dinero, hijo?

JOHNNY: Si, 'Apá, I got it. (JOHNNY *and* CECILIA *walk over to la* MUERTE.) One ticket, please.

MUERTE: Where to?

JOHNNY: Vietnam. I mean, Oakland.

MUERTE: Round trip or one way?

JOHNNY: One way.

MUERTE: Right. One way. (*Applies more make-up.*) (JOHNNY *gets his ticket and he and* CECILIA *start back toward his parents.* JOHNNY *stops abruptly and glances back at la* MUERTE, *who has already shifted positions.*)

CECILIA: What's wrong?

JOHNNY: Nothing. (*They join the parents.*)

MUERTE: For a half an hour, then, they exchange small talk and trivialties, repeating some of the things that have been said several times before. Cecilia promises Johnny she will be true to him and wait until he returns. Then it's time to go. "The Oakland-Vietnam Express is now receiving passengers at gate number four. All aboard, please."

JOHNNY: That's my bus.

MAMA: Ay, m'ijito.

PAPA: Cuídate mucho, pues, ¿eh, hijo?

JOHNNY: No se apure, jefe.

CECILIA: I love you, Johnny. (*She embraces him.*)

MUERTE: The Oakland-Vietnam Express is in the final boarding stages. All aboard, please. And thanks for going Greyhound.

JOHNNY: ¡Ya me voy! (*Embraces all around, weeping, last goodbyes, etc.* JOHNNY *exits. Then parents exit.* MAMA *and* CECILIA *are crying.*)

MUERTE: (*Sings.*) Adiós, Adiós
Lucero de mis noches
Dijo un soldado al pie de una ventana

Me voy, me voy
Pero no llores, angel mía
Que volveré mañana . . . So *JOHNNY* left for Vietnam, never to return. He didn't want to go and yet he did. It never crossed his mind to refuse. How could he refuse the gobierno de los Estados Unidos? How could he refuse his family? Besides, who wants to go to prison? And there was always the chance he'd come back alive . . . wounded maybe, but alive. So he took a chance and lost. But before he died, he saw many things in Vietnam; he had his eyes opened. He wrote his mother about them. (JOHNNY *and la* MAMA *enter at opposite sides of the stage.* JOHNNY *is in full battle gear. His face is now a skull.*)

JOHNNY: Dear jefita.

MAMA: Querido hijo.

JOHNNY: I am writing this letter.

MAMA: Recibí tu carta.

JOHNNY: To tell you I'm okay.

MAMA: Y doy gracias a los cielos que estás bien.

JOHNNY: How's everybody over there?

MAMA: Pos aquí todos estamos bien también, gracias a Dios.

JOHNNY: 'Amá, there's a lot happening here that I didn't know about before. I don't know if I'm allowed to write about it, pero voy a hacer la lucha. Yesterday we attacked a small village near some rice paddies. We had orders to kill everybody because they were supposed to be V-C's, comunistas. We entered the small pueblito and my buddies comenzaron a disparar. I saw one of them kill an old man and an old lady. My sergeant killed a small boy about seven years old, then he shot his mother or some woman that came running up crying. Blood was everywhere. I don't remember what happened after that, but my sergeant ordered me to start shooting. I think I did. May God forgive me for what I did, but I never wanted to come over here. They say we have to do it to defend our country.

MAMA: Hijo, me da tristeza con lo que nos escribes. Hablé con tu padre y también se puso muy triste, pero dice que así es la guerra. Tu recuerda que estás peleando con comunistas. Tengo una vela prendida allá por donde andas y que te regrese a nuestros brazos bueno y sano.

JOHNNY: 'Amá, I had a dream la otra noche. I dreamed I was breaking into one of the hooches, así le decimos a las casas de los vietnameses. I went in firing my M-16 porque sabía que el village estabe controlado por los gooks. I killed three of them right away, but when I looked down it was mi 'Apá, el carnalillo and you, jefita. I don't know how much more I can stand. Please tell Sapo and all the vatos how it's like over here. Don't let them . . . (*La* MUERTE *fires a gun, shooting* JOHNNY *in the head. He falls. La* MAMA *screams without looking at* JOHNNY.)

MUERTE: Johnny was killed in action, November, 1965, at Chuy Lai. His body lay in the field for two days and then it was taken to the beach and placed in a freezer, a converted portable food locker. Two weeks later he was shipped home for burial. (*La* MUERTE *straightens out* JOHNNY'*s body. Takes his helmet, rifle, etc.* EL PAPA, LA MAMA, *the* HERMANO, CECILIA *file past and gather around the body, taps play.*)

Bernabé

Characters:

Bernabé
Madre
El Primo
El Tío/El Sol
Torres/La Luna
Consuelo/La Tierra

The action takes place in a rural town in the San Joaquin Valley of California. The time is the early 1960s. It is summer — not a cloud in the sky, not a breeze in the air. The crops lie majestically over the landscape, over the immensity of the fecund earth. The valley is sweltering under the heat. The sun is lord and master.

Rising abruptly on the flatness of the land is Burlap, California — a small squat town not picturesque enough to be called a village, too large to be a labor camp — population 2,100, one of hundreds of similar tank towns that dot the long flat immensity of the valley, covered with dust and crankcase oil. The town has a Main Street, the commercial center of town, consisting of a gas station, general store, bank, hardware, cafe, Mexican show, and Torres Bar & Hotel. Amid these business establishments are empty lots littered with debris.

This is the world of Bernabé, a mentally-retarded farm worker in his early thirties touched with cosmic madness. The world of man he inhabits judges him insane but harmless — a source of amusement and easy stoop labor. In his own world, however — a world of profoundly elemental perceptions — he is a human being living in direct relationship to earth, moon, sun, and stars.

The set, then, is necessarily abstract — a design that blends myth and reality — the paradoxical vision of a cosmic idiot simply known as Bernabé. For he is a man who draws his full human worth not from the tragicomic daily reality of men, but from the collective, mythical universality of Mankind.

ONE

Midday: a scorcher in the San Joaquin Valley. Under an infinite pale blue sky, the dusty streets of Burlap, California are empty. No signs of life. Near Torres Bar & Hotel, BERNABE comes walking down the hot sidewalk at a steady clip. He is followed at some distance by his MADRE. Holding a transistor radio to his ear, BERNABE is listening to Tex-Mex music, oblivious to the heat.

MADRE: (*Stopping.*) Bernabé . . . (BERNABE *keeps going.*) Berna-BEH! (BERNABE *stops with a sly grin.*)

BERNABE: What?

MADRE: Wait . . . ¡Ay, Dios — this heat! (MADRE *waddles forward, sweating and gasping for air — a wizened vision of old age in black, with a shawl wrapped tightly around her head.*)

BERNABE: (*Rudely.*) What do you want?

MADRE: Don't go so fast, hijo. You leave me behind.

BERNABE: Well, step on it, you old bag.

MADRE: (*Angered.*) Don't be ill-bred, hombre! I don't know why you have to get so far ahead of me. What if I fall down, eh? Is that what you want — to see me dead in the streets?

BERNABE: (*Grumbling.*) . . . always dying of something.

MADRE: (*Sharply.*) ¿Qué?

BERNABE: Nothing.

MADRE: (*Fiercely.*) Be careful how you speak to me, eh? I'm your madre! Do you want the ground to open up and swallow you? That's what happens to sons who don't respect their mothers. The earth opens up and swallows them alive, screaming to the heavens!

BERNABE: (*Looking down.*) La tierra? . . . Chale, not me. (*We hear a distant drone high above. Distracted, BERNABE looks up at the sky. Smiling.*) Look . . . an airplane. It's a crop duster.

MADRE: (*Hitting him.*) Aren't you listening to me, hombre? I'm getting too old to be out chasing you in the streets — and in this hot sun! Dios mío, you should feel this headache I'm suffering. ¿Sabes qué? You better go on to the store without me. Here. (*She pulls out a small money purse and turns away, digging out coins. BERNABE peeks over her shoulder.*) Get back. (*BERNABE backs off. MADRE unfolds a ten dollar bill and hands it to him preciously.*) Take this. Buy some eggs, a pound of coffee, and a dozen tortillas. Do you think you can remember that?

BERNABE: (*Nodding.*) Eggs . . . coffee . . . tortillas. (*Pause.*) No pan dulce?

MADRE: No! And be careful with the change, eh? Don't let them cheat you. God knows what we're going to do till you find work. (*CONSUELO comes down the sidewalk, heading for the bar. BERNABE ogles her the moment she appears. MADRE scandalized.*) ¡Válgame Dios! Bernabé, turn around!

BERNABE: (*Grinning.*) ¿Por qué?

MADRE: ¡Qué importa! (*She turns him around. CONSUELO pauses for a second, smiling cynically, then exits into Torres Bar.*) Shameless viejas! ¡Descaradas! Don't ever let me catch you going into the cantinas, Bernabé — the shame would kill me! Andale, pues, get to the store. Go on . . . (*MADRE starts to exit. BERNABE pauses and picks up an empty beer can on the street.*)

BERNABE: Oiga, can I buy me . . . (*Looks at the beer can and hides it.*) . . . an ice cream?

MADRE: (*Turning.*) No, no, no! Qué ice cream ni qué mugre! There's no money for sweets. And if you see Señor Torres, the labor contractor, ask him for work. Tell him your leg is fine now. Get going! (BERNABE *starts to go, and* MADRE *exits in the opposite direction.* BERNABE *stops, once she is out of sight, and comes back to the bar. He crouches in the doorway looking in, as* EL PRIMO *and* TORRES *come down the sidewalk from the other side.*)

TORRES: So how was Tijuana?

PRIMO: A toda eme, boss.

TORRES: No problems, eh?

PRIMO: (*Cool and secretive.*) Chale. They had the carga waiting, I slipped them la lana, and I came back de volada. I got the stuff with me . . . fine shit, boss. The girls'll dig it.

TORRES: Let's go inside.

PRIMO: Orale.

TORRES: (*Spotting* BERNABE.) Well, well — look who's here. Your cousin! (*He kicks* BERNABE *playfully.*)

BERNABE: (*Jumping.*) ¡Ay! Baboso, hijo de la . . .

TORRES: (*Laughing.*) Don't get mad, loco.

PRIMO: (*Feeling bad.*) He's only playing with you, primo.

TORRES: ¿Qué pues? Aren't you going to say hello?

BERNABE: (*Uneasy.*) Hello, Torres.

TORRES: (*In a joking mood.*) Say, Eddie, did you know Bernabé has himself an old lady?

PRIMO: (*Humoring him.*) No, really, cousin?

BERNABE: (*Surprised.*) How do you know?

TORRES: The whole town knows. You've been sleeping with her.

PRIMO: No, really? (BERNABE *smiles mysteriously.*) Who is it, cousin? La Betty?

BERNABE: No.

PRIMO: La fat Mary?

BERNABE: (*Laughing.*) Chale.

PRIMO: Who, pues?

TORRES: Who else? The old lady who still gives him chi-chi. His mamá! (TORRES *laughs boisterously.*)

PRIMO: (*Offended.*) Orale, boss, you're laughing at my tía, man.

TORRES: Just kidding, hombre. ¿Qué traes? (*Getting back to business.*) Bueno, Bernabé, we got work to do. Let's go, Eddie.

PRIMO: Ahi te watcho, cousin. (TORRES *and* PRIMO *start to go into the bar.*)

TORRES: Está más loco . . .

BERNABE: (*Boldly.*) Hey, Torres!

TORRES: (*Stopping.*) What? (*Long pause.* BERNABE *searches for words.*)

PRIMO: What is it, primo?

BERNABE: (*Smiling slyly.*) I wanna be with my ruca.

PRIMO: Your ruca? What ruca?

BERNABE: The one that's right here.

TORRES: Here in my cantina?

BERNABE: No, here outside.

PRIMO: The sidewalk's empty, ese.

BERNABE: (*Insanely vague.*) The sidewalk's cement. She's over here . . . where the ground is . . . and out in the fields . . . and in the hills. (*Looking up.*) She loves the rain.

TORRES: (*Laughing.*) ¿Sabes qué? Something tells me this idiot wants to go upstairs.

PRIMO: (*Smiling.*) You mean — to visit Connie?

TORRES: He's got the itch. Isn't that it, Bernabé? You want one of my chamacas?

BERNABE: No!

TORRES: ¿Cómo que no? Your tongue's hanging out, loco. Look, if you tell me what you want, I'll get it for you. Compliments of the house.

BERNABE: With my ruca?

TORRES: The one you like.

BERNABE: (*Pause.*) I want a job.

TORRES: (*Puzzled.*) Job?

BERNABE: In the fields.

PRIMO: (*Laughs.*) He's got you now, Torres! You're gonna have to give him a chamba. The cousin's not as crazy as you think!

BERNABE: (*Laughs.*) Simón, I ain't crazy.

TORRES: (*Scoffing.*) You can't work with that crooked leg of yours.

BERNABE: It's okay now.

TORRES: And what about your head, loco? I can't have you throwing another fit and falling off the truck. Five men couldn't handle you.

PRIMO: Aliviánate, boss — it was only a heat stroke. Besides, Bernabé's the best swamper you ever had. How many potato sacks did you load last year, cousin? Two hundred, five hundred, mil?

BERNABE: Vale madre, mil!

PRIMO: A thousand sacos a day, man!

BERNABE: How about it, Torres?

TORRES: (*Shaking his head.*) Ni modo, Quasimodo. Tell your mother to try the Welfare.

BERNABE: I need money to buy la tierra.

TORRES: What tierra?

BERNABE: This one. Here and there and all over.

PRIMO: (*Humoring him.*) You wanna buy a ranchito?

BERNABE: (*Emphatically.*) No, a big rancho — with lots of tierra! All the tierra on earth. She's all mine.

TORRES: Yours?

BERNABE: My woman. We're gonna get married.

TORRES: (*Bursting out laughing.*) Pinche loco! Vámonos, Eddie. His woman! What this idiot needs is a vieja. (*He exits laughing.*)

PRIMO: Llévatela suave, primo. (PRIMO *exits. Long pause.*

BERNABE *kneels on the earth*.)
BERNABE: (*Slyly*.) Tierra, they think I'm crazy. But you know
I love you. (*Looks around*.) See you tonight, eh? . . . like
always. (*He kisses the ground and exits*.)

TWO

The scene is above and below the earth. Above,
BERNABE's *house, a small unpainted shack, sits back from the*
street on a narrow lot. Below, BERNABE *sits in a hole in the*
ground covered with planks, lighting candles to a sexy Aztec
goddess pictured on a calendar from Wong's Market. MADRE
emerges from the house. It is sundown.

MADRE: (*Calling*.) Bernabé? Bernabé, come and eat! Válgame
Dios, where is this hombre? BER-NA-BE! (BERNABE
ignores her. EL PRIMO *enters on the street*.)
PRIMO: Buenas tardes, tía. What's wrong? Lose Bernabé
again?
MADRE: No, qué lose! He hides just to make me suffer. Have
you seen him, hijo?
PRIMO: This morning, outside the cantina.
MADRE: (*Alarmed*.) La cantina?
PRIMO: I mean, the store, tía. The Chinaman's supermarket.
MADRE: (*Relieved*.) Pues, sí. I sent him to buy a few things for
me. I have a week now with a headache that won't go away.
If you only knew, hijo—how much I suffer and worry. Our
rent is almost up, and Bernabé without work. (*Pause*.) You
do have a job, no m'ijo?
PRIMO: (*Nods*.) I'm working with Torres.
MADRE: Ay, pos sí, ¿no? They say that Señor Torres is rich.
He always has money.
PRIMO: Almost all the men in town are unemployed, tía. There
won't be anything till the picking starts. Look, let me lend

you ten bucks.

MADRE: (*Self-righteous.*) No, Eduardo. What would your mother say? May God forbid it. I know my sister only too well. When it's about money, she's an owl. No, no, no!

PRIMO: (*Holding out a ten spot.*) Here, tía.

MADRE: No, hijo, gracias.

PRIMO: Andele. Take it. (*He tries to put the money in her hand.*)

MADRE: (*Folding her arms.*) No, no — y no!

PRIMO: (*Shrugging.*) Well . . .

MADRE: (*Quickly.*) Well, okay, pues! (MADRE *snatches the ten dollars with lightning reflexes and stuffs it in her bosom. hypocritically.*) And how is your madrecita?

PRIMO: Fine, like always.

MADRE: Gracias a Dios. Bueno, if you see m'ijo, send him straight home, eh? I don't know what will become of him. One of these days they'll put him in the crazy house, then what will I do?

PRIMO: Try not to worry, tía. Adiós. (MADRE *exits into her house.* PRIMO *starts to move on.* EL TIO *enters down the street.*)

TIO: ¡Oye, sobrino! Eddie!

PRIMO: Orale, tío — how you been?

TIO: Pos, ¿cómo? Hung-over. Oye, you wouldn't happen to have two bits? Un tostón — for the cure, you know? With 35 cents I can buy me a mickey y ya 'stuvo. (PRIMO *gives him the money.*) N'ombre! That's a real nephew. Say, I couldn't help notice you slipped some money to my little sister, eh?

PRIMO: A few bolas. So what?

TIO: (*Scratching his head.*) No, nothing, but I bet you she didn't even say gracias, right? Sure, don't deny it! Don't be a sucker, Guaro — haven't I told you? That old dried prune don't appreciate nothing. Look at me. How many years did I bust my ass in the fields to support her, her idiot son, and your own sweet mother who I love more than anybody? You know, when I go over to your house, your 'amá never fails to offer me a cup of coffee, a plate of beans — vaya, whatever, no? But this other miserable sister I got won't even give me a glass of water. Instead she tells me to get the hell on my way, because she has to feed Bernabé, and she don't like nobody to watch him eat! (PRIMO *laughs*.) Isn't that so? That's how she is.

PRIMO: Orale, pues, tío. And speaking of the primo, you seen him?

TIO: (*Suspiciously.*) ¿Por qué? Is that old coyota looking for him? ¡Qué caray! (*Pause.*) Look, you know where the poor loco is? — but don't tell his madre, eh? . . . he's right there, in the field by his house.

PRIMO: The empty lot?

TIO: Sí, hombre, the little llano where the kids play. He's got a hole there he dug into the ground, see? That's where he crawls in and hides. At first he used to get into rock fights with the snot-noses, but lately he's been waiting till dark to go down there, so nobody bothers him.

PRIMO: (*Puzzled.*) How do you know all this, tío?

TIO: I've seen him. He disappears like a gopher and don't come out for two or three hours.

PRIMO: What does he do?

TIO: ¡Sabrá Judas! I even went and got into the hole myself once — when he was downtown with his madre, but I didn't see nothing . . . except for the dirt, soft and warm — like he crawls in and squirms around it.

PRIMO: In the dirt?

TIO: What else is there?

PRIMO: (*Pause.*) Chale. It can't be.

TIO: ¿Qué?

PRIMO: Forget it. He's not that crazy.

TIO: Sure he's crazy. Completely nuts.

PRIMO: Can he be that far gone?

TIO: Cracked and eaten by burros! What's on your mind?

PRIMO: Just something he told me and Torres this morning.

TIO: (*Pause.*) What?

PRIMO: Nothing much. It's impossible.

TIO: (*Exasperated.*) Well, what is it, hombre? You got me standing on my toenails!

PRIMO: (*Pause.*) He said he has a girlfriend.

TIO: Girlfriend?

PRIMO: La Tierra.

TIO: You mean the dirt?

PRIMO: (*Nods.*) And that they're gonna get married.

TIO: (*Pause.*) And you think he . . .? No, hombre! He can't be that crazy!

PRIMO: Didn't I tell you?

TIO: (*Pause.*) A hole in the ground? (*Angered.*) Pos, mira qué loco tan cochino, hombre! How can he be doing such a dirty thing? Fucking idiot!

PRIMO: Easy, tío.

TIO: It's disgusting, Guaro. He's not your nephew.

PRIMO: He's a cousin.

TIO: Pos, ¡ahi 'ta! He's disgracing the whole family. We got the same blood, hombre. Chihuahua! What's his madre going to say if she finds him out? I bet you she suspects something already.

PRIMO: Chale.

TIO: Sí, señor. You think I don't know my own sister?

MADRE: (*Offstage.*) Berna-beh!

TIO: Listen! Here she comes again. (PRIMO *and* TIO *hide in the shadows, as* MADRE *re-enters. She spots* BERNABE*'s hole in the ground and approaches it suspiciously. Lifting a plank, she suddenly spots him.*)

MADRE: (*Gasping.*) Bernabé? Por Dios, come out of there!

PRIMO: She's got him.

TIO: ¡Pobre loco! He's going to get it now. (MADRE *starts tearing off the planks, as* BERNABE *cowers in his hole.*)

MADRE: ¡Ave María Purísima! ¡Virgencita pura, ayúdame! (PRIMO *and* TIO *rush to the hole.*)

TIO: Quihubo pues, sister? What's the matter?

MADRE: Don't bother me now, Teodoro! I've got too many troubles.

TIO: Huy, pos—what's new?

MADRE: Don't even talk to me, hombre! You can be a disgraceful wino if you want, but I have to look out for m'ijo!

PRIMO: Did you find Bernabé, tía?

MADRE: Sí, hijo! Look where he is—in a filthy hole! Come out of there, Bernabé!

BERNABE: (*Refusing to come out.*) CHALE!

MADRE: ¡Sal de ahí te digo!

BERNABE: (*Cursing.*) ¡Vieja cabrona, píntese!

MADRE: (*Shocked.*) What? ¡Bendito sea Dios! Did you hear what he called me?

TIO: (*Smiling.*) What's he doing?

MADRE: (*Pushing him back.*) None of your business! You up here—staggering in the streets, and my son down there risking death, verdad?

TIO: What death? Stop exaggerating.

MADRE: (*Fuming.*) Exaggerating? Exaggerating! And if the ground falls on top of him, what can happen, eh? Dios mío, he'll suffocate! Do you hear me, Bernabé? Come out of that dark, ugly hole!

PRIMO: The tía's right, primo. Come on out.

MADRE: Talk to him, Eduardo. Please! Before I die of the . . .

TIO: Exaggeration.

MADRE: (*Lashing at him.*) ¡Cállate el hocico! Just get out of here, sabes? Leave!

TIO: You leave! Pos, mira, qué chirrión.

MADRE: Come out, Bernabé! ¡Ahorita mismo!

PRIMO: (*Reaching in.*) Come on, primo.

BERNABE: (*Shaking his head.*) What are you going to do to me?

MADRE: Nothing. Just come out.

PRIMO: Grab my hand, ese. (BERNABE *grabs* PRIMO's *hand*

and slowly emerges from the pit.)

BERNABE: (*Fearful.*) Are you going to hit me, oiga?

MADRE: Come on, Bernabé!

BERNABE: (*Coming out.*) If you lay a finger on me, I'll kick your ass.

MADRE: (*Gasps.*) ¡Válgame Dios, Bernabé! (*She grabs him.*) Now I am going to hit you, for your filthy mouth! ¡Malcriado! (*She beats him.*)

BERNABE: (*Cowering.*) ¡Ay! ¡No! ¡No, mamá!

TIO: That's enough, let him alone!

PRIMO: Don't hit him, tía.

MADRE: (*Incensed.*) Stay out of this—both of you! Bernabé's my son and I have the right to punish him. (*She hits him again.*)

TIO: But he's a man. Not a kid! (*Stopping her.*)

MADRE: I don't care! I'm his madre. And so long as God gives me life, I'll go on punishing him when he does wrong! Let go of me!

BERNABE: (*Weeping like a child.*) I didn't do nothing!

MADRE: Sí, nothing! You think I'm blind, eh? What were you doing in that hole? You think I don't know what dirty things you do in there? I can just imagine! But one of these nights the moon is going to come down and swallow you alive—¡por cochino!

BERNABE: (*With fear.*) No, 'amá, la luna no.

MADRE: Yes, you'll see! ¡Vamos, ándale! Into the house! ¡Ave María Santísima! (MADRE *exits with* BERNABE, *pulling him by the hair.* PRIMO *and* TIO *look at each other sorrowfully.*)

TIO: Pobre loco.

PRIMO: She treats him like a kid.

TIO: That's what he is. You saw him—he really believes the moon can come down and swallow him. But I know what you mean. In a few weeks, he'll be in the fields, working and sweating like an animal. And do you think my sister appreciates it? No, hombre, she rents him like a burro!

PRIMO: Say, tío—how old is Bernabé?

TIO: Pos, lemme see . . . thirty four? No, wait . . . thirty seven!

PRIMO: And how many girlfriends has he had?

TIO: Are you serious?

PRIMO: Simón. (*Pause.*) None, am I right?

TIO: Ninguna.

PRIMO: ¡Orale! Then it's not craziness.

TIO: What?

PRIMO: All th funny stuff about la tierra and the hole and everything, tío. Figure it out. (*Pause.*) Look, will you help me do the cousin a favor?

TIO: Like what?

PRIMO: Pos, ya sabe. You know Consuelo, the hot momma that works over in Torres Club?

TIO: ¿La p . . .?

PRIMO: ¡Simón, la chavalona!

TIO: No, Guaro, I don't get into those things no more.

PRIMO: So what? Look, go to the club and tell her to wait for me in one hour. Tell her Eddie wants to talk to her. Understand?

TIO: And why don't you go?

PRIMO: Because I'm bringing the primo.

TIO: (*Scoffing.*) Oh, sure. His madre's gonna let him go straight to the cantina! Forget it, sobrino. You're a bigger fool than I thought.

PRIMO: (*Smiling.*) You just leave the tía to me. She and I get along fine. If I tell her I'm taking Bernabé to see Torres about a job, no hay pedo. I'll have him there. ¿Juega?

TIO: Pos, qué caray, okay pues. ¡Juega!

PRIMO: (*Taking out money.*) Then here—have a few cold beers while you wait for us.

TIO: (*Taking the money eagerly.*) ¡Ay, chirrión! You mean I have to wait?

PRIMO: Don't you want to see your nephew happy?

TIO: What nephew? That pitiful idiot?

PRIMO: He's not such an idiot, tío. You'll see. Bueno, trucha pues. Torres Club, eh? Around nine. (PRIMO *and* TIO *start to go in opposite directions.*)

TIO: (*Stopping.*) ¡Epa! And what's the name of the . . . ?

PRIMO: Consuelo. She's got the big chamorrotes (thighs).

TIO: Pos, you ought to know. I don't.

PRIMO: (*Laughing.*) Orale, pues, ahí nos watchamos later. I'm going to eat with the tía. (*Starts to go again.*)

TIO: (*Stopping again.*) ¡Oye! And if Bernabé doesn't want to . . . tú sabes . . .

PRIMO: Then the favor's for you, tío. (*Exits.*)

TIO: (*Starts to exit.*) Ha! For me . . . (*Stops. Reconsiders, tilts head, smiles.*) Consuelo, eh? (*He exits.*)

THREE

Torres Club. Outside in the back alley. BERNABE *comes out of the cantina with a beer can. The moon is bright.*

BERNABE: (*Looking down.*) Tierra? It's me . . . out here in this alley. See, that's Torres' cantina . . . Look—a cerveza. You know what? My primo went and covered the hole where we get together. Mi 'amá sent him. But who cares, huh? It's just some boards. Tomorrow I'll take 'em off! Anyway, you're here, and over there, and way over there. And right, right here. We're always together! (*Laughs and kisses the earth.* TORRES *enters. Sees* BERNABE, *laughs to himself, shaking his head.* BERNABE *scoops up a handful of dirt.*)

TORRES: Oye, oye, stop feeling her up!

BERNABE: (*Startled.*) Uh?

TORRES: (*Laughs.*) Don't get scared, loco. It's me. How's the girlfriend, okay?

BERNABE: Simón, okay. (*He rises.*)

TORRES: Nice and cool, eh? Pos, qué suave. Chihuahua, it's hot, hombre! The sun went down and the night stayed hot. What are you doing here so late?

BERNABE: Nothing. (*Hiding his handful of dirt.*)

TORRES: And that beer?

BERNABE: My primo bought it for me. We came to look for work.

TORRES: So where's Eddie? Inside?

BERNABE: (*Nodding.*) Talking to Torres.

TORRES: Oh sí, eh? And who am I? La Luna?

BERNABE: (*Startled.*) Chale.

TORRES: (*Laughs.*) No, ¿verdad? There's the moon up there. Look how big she is! I wonder if she's jealous? The moon's a woman too, eh? Or maybe not. Maybe he's the brother of your ruca. Watch it, Bernabé, he's gonna take her away!

BERNABE: ¡Pura madre! Nobody can take her away!

TORRES: Well, don't get pissed.

BERNABE: She's mine. (*Looks at his handful.*)

TORRES: (*Tongue in cheek.*) Then tell that to the gabachos. See if they give her back.

BERNABE: What gabachos?

TORRES: The landowners, manito. Banks, corporations.

BERNABE: They ain't nobody.

TORRES: (*Pause.*) Hey — and if I wanted the land too, Bernabé? What do I do?

BERNABE: (*Laughs.*) Aguántate. You just wait!

TORRES: But she's my mamá.

BERNABE: ¿La tierra?

TORRES: Sure. She's your momma too.

BERNABE: Up yours! She's not my mother.

TORRES: Bueno, your hot momma, then. But look how the ranchers treat her, hombre. They sell her whenever they feel like it — to the highest bidder! See those fields over there? I just bought 'em yesterday. I own the ground under your feet too. All the lots on this street. And I got more on the other side of the barrio. Check it out. But you know what, loco? I'll rent her to you. (*Laughs.*) Give me a few bucks, and I'll let you have her—for the night! (BERNABE *is genuinely puzzled. He finds* TORRES*'s reasoning totally nonsensical.*)

BERNABE: Say, Torres, you're even crazier than me! (*Laughs.*) ¡Ah, qué Torres!

TIO: (*Entering.*) ¡Oye tú! Where you been?

BERNABE: Right here.

TIO: What are you up to, hombre? Why did you leave the bar? (*Spots* TORRES.) Oh, buenas noches, Señor Torres.

TORRES: Buenas . . . (*Suspicious.*) What's up, Teodoro?

TIO: (*Nervous.*) No, nothing, this burro . . . I don't know why I got into this! Eddie brought him here . . . to do him a favor . . . (*Barking at* BERNABE.) Let's go inside, ándale! Your cousin already went up with the vieja. He said to get ready.

TORRES: No, hombre! He's going in with Connie?

TIO: Pos sí, if she lets him in.

TORRES: (*Smiles.*) Sure she'll let him. She does what I tell her.

TIO: My nephew's already talking her into it.

TORRES: So you're going to get laid, eh Bernabé?

BERNABE: (*Getting scared.*) I want another beer.

TIO: There's no more. Go do your duty!

TORRES: Don't rush him, hombre. This is an occasion. Come on in. So you're finally going to get married, eh loco?

TIO: ¡Qué pinche vergüenza! (*Exits.*)

FOUR

Torres Club—interior. The upstairs hallway of a cheap hotel. PRIMO *enters, his arm around* CONSUELO.

PRIMO: Orale, Connie, gracias for doing me this favor, eh?

CONSUELO: It's no favor, man. You gotta pay me.

PRIMO: Simón, but the vato's muy especial, you know?

CONSUELO: Who is this jerk?

PRIMO: My cousin.

CONSUELO: Who?

PRIMO: Bernabé.

CONSUELO: (*Nonplussed.*) You mean . . . el loquito del pueblo? Sorry, Eddie, I'm sorry, but no dice.

PRIMO: ¿Por qué no?

CONSUELO: Because, porque no. How do I know what he's gonna do? Because he's crazy, that's why!

PRIMO: He's not that loco, chula. He just needs a little break.

CONSUELO: Well, it's not me, man.

PRIMO: Look, it's no big deal. I'm asking you to do the vato a favor. He's my primo — sure he's missing a few marbles, but so what? He's got everything else. Andale, chula — just for a little bit. I promised him — it's his birthday.

CONSUELO: (*Pause.*) Give me fifteen bucks and he's on.

PRIMO: Fifteen bolas? What are you — gold-plated down there? (CONNIE *starts to go.*) No, look, Connie — don't be that way. Besides, all I got are nine bills, see? Here. (*Gives her the money.*)

CONSUELO: (*Takes it reluctantly.*) Bueno, okay. But just one turn on the merry-go-round and that's it. Where's the loco at?

PRIMO: He's coming with el tío — they had a beer first.

CONSUELO: Tío?

PRIMO: Teodoro.

CONSUELO: That winito's your tío?

PRIMO: Simón, and also Bernabé's.

CONSUELO: And is his mamá here too?

PRIMO: Chale, what's with you?

CONSUELO: Naranjas, corazón. Okay, send him in, pues. (CONSUELO *exits into her room.*)

TIO: (*Offstage.*) Guaro?

PRIMO: Orale, tío — up here.

TIO: (*Offstage.*) Here comes Lover Boy . . . Drooling in his shorts! Is she ready?

PRIMO: And set to go.

TIO: (*Enters puffing.*) Híjole, la chicharra, hombre! It took long enough to get up here. Where's the bride?

PRIMO: In her room.

TIO: (*Looking.*) Ah, pos sí, I recognize the place.

PRIMO: Just like old times, eh tío?

TIO: Huy, what can I say, sobrino? I personally broke in this hotel. Every payday, I couldn't keep my nose out of here. They had some big fine things up here in those days.

PRIMO: And Bernabé?

TIO: (*Turning.*) He was right behind . . . Adiós, where did he go? There he is! See? ¡Andale, oyes! Don't hide. Come on up.

BERNABE: (*Offstage.*) For what?

TIO: For what? Pos—what do you think? It's payday. Are you scared?

BERNABE: (*Offstage.*) NO!

PRIMO: All right, ese, the ruca's waiting for you.

BERNABE: (*Entering.*) Where?

PRIMO: In there. It's la Connie, the one who was at the bar? La watchates? The fine buns and the big legs? (BERNABE *laughs.*) Simón qué yes, verdad? She's ready, she's willing, and she's able, carnal. So get in there. Go get it!

BERNABE: (*Playing dumb.*) What?

PRIMO: You know, loco. (BERNABE *laughs lasciviously. He looks at his* PRIMO *and* TIO, *then hesitantly starts toward* CONSUELO'*s room. He reaches the door and is about to go in, when he stops suddenly and turns grinning idiotically.*)

BERNABE: (*Backing off.*) Chale.

PRIMO: Nel, primo—don't chicken out, man. She's all set. Andale!

BERNABE: (*Shaking his head.*) No, she'll swallow me.

TIO: Swallow you!

BERNABE: La Luna. For being dirty.

PRIMO: That's bullshit, primo. Come on, you saw Connie. You liked what you saw, right?

BERNABE: Yeah.

PRIMO: Well then? Go see it all.

BERNABE: Not now.

PRIMO: Why not?

BERNABE: I don't feel like it.

TIO: You felt like it downstairs.

BERNABE: (*Turning.*) I want another beer first.

TIO: Later—afterward.

PRIMO: You have to go in now, primo. She's waiting for you. Besides, I already paid her . . . twenty bucks. Okay?

BERNABE: I don't think so.

TIO: But didn't you hear, hombre. He already paid the vieja!

BERNABE: I don't give a shit. I don't want that vieja!

TIO: Bueno, if he's not going in . . . (*Pause.*) He's not going in. Take the idiot home, and that's it.

CONSUELO: (*At her door.*) Eddie? Oye, Eddie? ¿Qué pasó, pues?

PRIMO: Hold it a second.

CONSUELO: Hold it yourself! Tell him to hurry. (*She retreats into her room.*)

PRIMO: You see? She wants you to go in.

TIO: And to hurry.

PRIMO: Come on, ese. I know you want to.

TIO: Sure, he wants to. ¡Está buenota, hombre! I wouldn't hold back.

BERNABE: Then, you get in there.

TIO: Don't be an idiot! Qué caray, I would if I could, but I can't no more. She's more than I can handle. Here, have a drink—to give you strength. (*Gives him a swig of his beer.*)

PRIMO: Okay, pues, get in there, cuz!

TIO: Be a man, m'ijo. (BERNABE *starts to move toward* CONSUELO's *door again. Cautiously, he is about to enter, but he stops and beats a retreat.*)

BERNABE: (*Backing off again.*) Chale, I can't!

TIO: (*Cursing.*) ¡Me lleva la . . . que me trajo! This is a jackass without a rope, hombre.

PRIMO: (*Giving up.*) Simón, let's go, pues.

BERNABE: Where we going?

PRIMO: Home to your chante.

BERNABE: Nel, I wanna booze it up.

TIO: We alreday boozed it up.

BERNABE: Just one.

TIO: (*Exasperated.*) N'ombre! This fool don't want a puta, he wants a peda. Better take him home, Guaro. Before he gets drunk.

BERNABE: I'm not going to get drunk, oiga!

PRIMO: Let's go, Bernabé.

BERNABE: No! I wanna stay here.

TIO: Your madre's waiting for you.

BERNABE: ¡Me importa madre! They're waiting for me here too.

TIO: (*Shoving him toward the door.*) Then, get in there!

BERNABE: (*Pause.*) No . . . she'll swallow me.

PRIMO: (*Tries to pull him.*) Let's go, ese.

BERNABE: No!

TIO: ¡Andale! Grab him! (PRIMO *and* TIO *grab* BERNABE.)

BERNABE: (*Resisting.*) No! Nooo! I wanna drink! I wanna viejaaa! I want la tierraaa! (CONSUELO *comes out of her room in a nightgown.*)

CONSUELO: Oye, oye, what's happening, Eddie?

PRIMO: Nothing. We're going.

CONSUELO: ¿Qué pasó? Isn't he coming in?

PRIMO: Chale.

TIO: He's crazy. (CONSUELO *comes up to* BERNABE, *mockingly wanton, sultrily flaunting her body before his gaping eyes.*)

CONSUELO: ¿Qué pasó, Bernabé? You don't want to come

with me? You know me, ¿qué no? I'm Consuelo — la Connie. Come on, gimme a little hug. (BERNABE *retreats.*) Andale, hombre — don't back away! Eddie tells me you like las chavalonas. Is that true, eh? Mira — gimme your hand like this . . . and now we put it here. (*She wraps his arm around her.* BERNABE *opens his fist — the handful of earth falls to the floor.*) Like novios, see? Do you want to dance? I have a record player in my room. Come on, let's go to the baile . . . (*She takes him to the door of her room.*) ¿Y ustedes? What are you gawking at? Get lost! Can't you see we're going on our honeymoon? (CONSUELO *laughs and closes the door, pulling in* BERNABE *with her.* PRIMO *approaches the dirt on the floor.*)

TIO: ¿Qué es eso? What did he drop?

PRIMO: Tierra . . . (*They look at each other.*) Come on, tío. I'll buy you a beer.

TIO: Let's go. This idiot nephew's driving me crazy! (*They exit.*)

FIVE

CONSUELO*'s room: darkness. A brief erotic silence, slowly punctuated by* CONSUELO*'s moans and the pounding of* BERNABE*'s heartbeat.*

CONSUELO: (*In the dark.*) Ay, papasito . . . Ay, ay, ¡AY!

BERNABE: (*Screaming.*) ¡AYYY!

CONSUELO: (*Pause.*) Bernabé?

BERNABE: ¡Quítate! ¡AYYYY!

CONSUELO: Shut up, hombre! ¿Qué tienes?

BERNABE: No, mamá, yo no hice nadaaaa!

CONSUELO: Are you going nuts on me?

BERNABE: Mamá! Mamáááá! (*Strobe light effect, slow to fast.* BERNABE *is backing away from* CONSUELO — *or at least the* MADRE *dressed in* CONSUELO*'s clothes. The*

effect is nightmarish.)
MADRE: (*As* CONSUELO.) ¿Qué tienes, papasito?
BERNABE: (*Backing off.*) No, nooooo!
MADRE: Naranjas, corazón. Don't you want to be with me? I'm
your girlfriend . . . tu novia. (*Changing into* MADRE.)
¡Pero también soy madre y te voy a pegar! ¡Por cochino!
¡Vente! ¡Vámonos pa' la casa! (*She grabs him by the hair.*)
BERNABE: (*Like a child.*) No, mami, noooo! (MADRE
changes into CONSUELO *and strokes* BERNABE's *head
and face, calming him down.*)
MADRE: (*As* CONSUELO.) Pero, ¿por qué no, bonito? You
know me, que no? I'm Consuelo, La Connie. Eddie tells me
you like las chavalonas. Don't you want me? Soy tu
novia . . . (*Back to* MADRE.) ¡Y por eso te voy a pegar! Soy
tu madre, y tengo derecho de castigarte mientras Dios me
preste vida. You want la tierra to swallow you alive? Come
with me!
BERNABE: (*Shoving her back.*) No, noo, no quierooo!
Tierraaaa! (BERNABE *runs out into the hallway. Lights up.
Strobe effect disappears.* PRIMO, TORRES, *and* TIO *come
running.*)
PRIMO: What's the matter, primo?
TORRES: ¡Oye, Connie! What the hell's going on, pues? (CON-
SUELO *comes out of her room, as herself.* BERNABE
screams.)
CONSUELO: Torres! Get this baboso out of here! ¡Sáquenlo!
PRIMO: What happen, chula?
CONSUELO: I don't know what happen. Está loco, ¿qué no
ves?
BERNABE: (*Terrified.*) ¡Yo no hice nada!
TORRES: Did he go in at least?
PRIMO: Sure he went in.
TIO: Se metió bien contento.
CONSUELO: I told you, Eddie! ¡Te dije!
PRIMO: Come on, primo. Let's go home.

BERNABE: (*Cries out in horror.*) No! Nooo! ¡Me pega! She'll hit me!

PRIMO: Who'll hit you?

BERNABE: (*Points at* CONSUELO.) ¡Mi 'amáááá!

TIO: This isn't your mother, suato!

CONSUELO: See what I mean. (BERNABE *screams.*)

TORRES: (*To* CONSUELO.) Don't talk to him, stupid! Keep your mouth shut!

CONSUELO: You bastard. This is all your fault! You think I like to do this?

TORRES: ¡Cállate el hocico!

CONSUELO: And you keep the money!

TORRES: Get into your room! (*He pushes her.*)

CONSUELO: (*Defiantly.*) Tell them! Tell 'em how you use the girls! And for what? Your pinche drugs?

TORRES: (*Slapping her around.*) I said shut your fucking mouth!

BERNABE: (*Reacting.*) No, nooo! MAMA! (*Rushes* TORRES.)

PRIMO: ¡Bernabé, cálmala!

TIO: Settle down, hombre!

TORRES: (BERNABE *on his back.*) Get him out of here!

PRIMO: We're trying, boss!

CONSUELO: Kick his ass, Bernabé!

TORRES: (*Pushing* CONSUELO.) I'm gonna get you!

BERNABE: (*Pounding on him.*) No, ¡déjala! Leave her alone! (PRIMO *and* TIO *struggle to take* BERNABE *off* TORRES.) PRIMO: Primo!

TIO: Bernabé!

BERNABE: She's mine! My woman is mine!

TORRES: ¡Quítenlo! Get him OFF OF ME! (*He falls.* CONSUELO *laughs.* BERNABE *is hysterical, totally out of it.* PRIMO *and* TIO *succeed in pulling him off* TORRES.)

BERNABE: ¡Lo maté! ¡LO MATE! I KILLED TORRES! (BERNABE *runs out.* TIO *starts to run after him.* PRIMO *helps* TORRES *on his feet.* CONSUELO *is still laughing.*)

TIO: (*Calling.*) Bernabé! Come back here, you idiot!

PRIMO: You okay, boss?

TORRES: ¿Pos, luego? Let me go.

TIO: ¡Oye, Guaro! The loco ran outside! What if he goes and tells his madre?

PRIMO: I don't understand what happened to him. What did you do?

CONSUELO: Don't ask me, man! It's not my fault if he thinks I'm his pinche madre!

TIO: (*To* PRIMO.) ¡Vámonos, hombre! We're gonna lose him!

PRIMO: Orale, let's go. Sorry, Torres. (*They exit.* CONSUELO *and* TORRES *are left behind.* CONSUELO *looks at* TORRES *and starts laughing. A deep bitter laugh, not without a certain satisfaction. She exits into her room.*)

TORRES: Goddamn whore! (*He exists.*)

SIX

El llano: night. There is a full moon, unseen, but casting an eery light on the earth. BERNABE *is at his hole, pulling off the boards. Suddenly, from the sky comes music.*

BERNABE: (*Crying out.*) ¡Tierraaa! I killed Torres! ¡Hijo 'e su tiznada madre! ¡LO MATE! (*Pause. He hears the danzón music.*) What's that? (*Stops. Fearfully looks at sky, sees moon.*) ¡La Luna! It's coming down! ¡Mamá, la lunaaa! (*Sobs like a child. Moonlight gathers into a spot focussed on him.* LA LUNA *enters, dressed like a Pachuco, 1942 style: Zoot suit, drapes, calcos, hat with feather, small chain, etc.*)

LUNA: Orale, pues, ese vato. No te escames. Soy yo, la Luna.

BERNABE: (*Wrapping himself into a ball.*) ¡No, chale!

LUNA: Control, ese. Ain't you Chicano? You're a vato loco.

BERNABE: (*Looks up slowly.*) I ain't loco.

LUNA: Oh, simón. I didn't mean it like that, carnal. Te estaba cabuliando. Watcha. If they don't like you the way you are, pos que tengan que, ¡pa' que se mantengan! ¡Con safos, putos! Shine 'em on, ese. Inside you know who you are. Can you dig it?

BERNABE: (*Feeling better.*) Simón.

LUNA: Pos a toda madre. (*Pause. Reaches into his pocket.*) Oye, like to do a little grifa? A good reefer will set you straight. You got any trolas? (*Finds match, lights joint for* BERNABE.) Alivian el esqueleto, carnal. Me and you are going to get bien locos tonight. Ahi te llevo. (*Grabs joint from* BERNABE.) No le aflojes. (BERNABE *gets joint again.*) Ese, you see them stars way up there? — some of them got some fine asses . . . (BERNABE *laughs.*) Say, I saw you go into Torres Club tonight. How was it?

BERNABE: (*Guilty.*) Okay.

LUNA: Simón, that Connie's a real mamasota, carnal. But tell me — a la bravota — why didn't you put it to her? Chicken? (BERNABE *throws the joint down.*) No, chale, don't tell me, pues. None of my beeswax. Here, no te agüites. (*Gives him back the joint.*) Oye, Bernabé, ¿sabes qué? I got a boner to pick with you, man. It's about my carnala.

BERNABE: Your carnala?

LUNA: Mi sister, loco. What you up to?

BERNABE: Nothing.

LUNA: Don't act pendejo, ese! I've been watching you get together almost every night. You dig me? She asked me to come down and see what's cooking. You just wanna get laid or what? She wants to make it forever, loco.

BERNABE: Forever?

LUNA: With you. Me la rayo. Watcha, let me call her. (*Calls.*) Oye, sister, come on! Somebody's waiting for you. (*Music accompanies the entrance of* LA TIERRA. *She emerges from the hole dressed as a soldadera [soldier woman of the Mexican Revolution, 1910] with a sombrero and cartridge belts.* BERNABE *is spellbound the moment he sees her. She stares at* BERNABE, *amazon and earth mother.*)

TIERRA: ¿Quién es?

LUNA: Pos, who? Your vato loco. Bernabé, this is my carnala. La Tierra.

TIERRA: Buenas noches, Bernabé. (BERNABE *makes a slight grunt, smiling idiotically.*) You don't know me? (BERNABE *is speechless and embarrassed.*)

LUNA: Orale, pues, carnal, say something. Don't tell me you're scared of her? (BERNABE *struggles to say something. His mind tries to form words. He ends up starting to laugh moronically, from helplessness.*)

TIERRA: (*Sharply.*) No, hombre, don't laugh! Speak to me seriously. Soy la tierra. (BERNABE *stares at her. A sudden realization strikes him and turns into fear. He screams and runs.*)

LUNA: ¡Epale! Where you going, loco? (*Stops* BERNABE *with a wave of his arm.*) Cálmala—be cool! There's nothing to be scared of. (*Pulls him toward* TIERRA.) Look at my carnala, see how a toda madre she looks in the moonlight... She loves you, man. Verdad, sister?

TIERRA: If he is a man. (BERNABE *is caught in a strange spell. He and* LA TIERRA *look at each other for a long moment.* LA LUNA *gets restless.*)

LUNA: Bueno, le dijo la mula al freno. You know what? I'm going to take a little spin around the stars—check up on the latest chisme. Oye, Bernabé, watch it with my sister, eh? Llévensela suave, pues. (*Exits.*)

TIERRA: (*Softly.*) What are you thinking, Bernabé?

BERNABE: (*Struggling to say something.*) I killed Torres.

TIERRA: (*Pushing him down.*) H'm, ¡qué pelado este! Weren't you thinking about me? Don't pride yourself. Torres isn't dead.

BERNABE: He's still alive?

TIERRA: Pos, luego. How were you going to kill him? With

your bare hands? Right now, he's in his bar laughing at you!

BERNABE: ¿Por qué?

TIERRA: Because he knows I belong to him. Not to you.

BERNABE: (*Incensed.*) Chale, you're mine!

TIERRA: And how am I yours, Bernabé? Where and when have you stood up for me? All your life you've worked in the fields like a dog — and for what? So others can get rich on your sweat, while other men lay claim to me? Torres says he owns me, Bernabé — what do you own? Nothing. (*Pause. BERNABE's head is down.*) Look at me, hombre! Soy la Tierra! Do you love me? Because if your love is true, then I want to be yours. (BERNABE *reaches out to embrace her.*) But not so fast, pelado! I'm not Consuelo, sabes? If you truly love me, you'll have to respect me for what I am, and then fight for me — ¡como los machos! Don't you know anything? Many men have died just to have me. Are you capable of killing those who have me . . . and do not love me, Bernabé?

BERNABE: You want me to kill?

TIERRA: To set me free. For I was never meant to be the property of any man — not even you . . . though it is your destiny to lie with me. (*She extends her hand. BERNABE goes to her. She pulls him down, and they lay down. He is almost going to embrace her, when* LA LUNA *comes back.*)

LUNA: Orale, stop right there! (BERNABE *sits up.*) ¿Qué, pues, nuez? Didn't I tell you to watch it with my sister? What were you doing, eh?

BERNABE: (*Rises.*) ¿Qué te importa, buey? (LA TIERRA *rises and stands to one side, observing silently but with strenth. BERNABE seems more self-possessed.*)

LUNA: Oye, so bravo all of a sudden?

BERNABE: You'd better leave, Luna!

LUNA: I'd better not, carnal!

BERNABE: Get out of here!

LUNA: Look at him, will you? Muy machote. What did you do

to him, sis?

BERNABE: ¡Lárgate! (*Pushes* LUNA.)

LUNA: Hey, man, watch the suit. I'm your camarada, remember? Almost your brother-in-law.

TIERRA: (*With power.*) Luna! Leave us in peace. He means me no harm.

LUNA: Pura madre, how do you know?

TIERRA: Because I know him. Since the very day of his birth, he has been innocent, and good. Others have laughed at him. But he has always come to my arms seeking my warmth. He loves me with an intensity most men cannot even imagine . . . for in his eyes I am woman . . . I am Madre . . .

LUNA: Simón — ¡pura madre!

TIERRA: Yet I'm forever Virgin. So leave us alone!

LUNA: Nel, sister. Qué virgen ni que madre. I know what you two are up to. Are you going to get married or what? Is this a one night stand?

TIERRA: That's up to Bernabé.

LUNA: What do you say, loco? Is this forever?

BERNABE: (*Pause.*) Simón.

LUNA: Pendejo.

TIERRA: Satisfied?

LUNA: Chale. You still need Jefe's blessing.

TIERRA: He'll grant it.

LUNA: Pos, you hope. First he's gotta meet Bernabé. You ready for Him, ese?

BERNABE: Who?

LUNA: El Mero Mero, loco. Su Papá. Mi Jefito. ¡EL SOL!

BERNABE: ¡¿Sol?!

LUNA: (*Turning.*) He's coming — watcha. It's almost dawn. ¿Sabes qué, ese? You better let me do the talking first. Me and the Jefe get along real suave. I'll tell Him you're Chicano, my camarada.

TIERRA: No, Luna.

LUNA: What?

161

TIERRA: He has a voice. Let him speak for himself.

LUNA: (*Shrugging.*) Orale, no hay pedo. But you know the Jefito.

TIERRA: You will have to face him, Bernabé. If you truly love me, then you should have no fear of my father. Speak to him with respect, but with courage. He has no patience with cowardly humans.

LUNA: ¡Al alba! Here he comes! Don't stare at his face too long, ese! He'll blind you! (*LA TIERRA and LA LUNA kneel before the place where the sun is rising. Indígena music: majestic flutes and drums. EL SOL rises in the guise of Tonatiuh, the Aztec Sun God. He speaks in a resounding voice.*)

SOL: Buenos días, mis hijos.

TIERRA: Buenos días, Papá.

LUNA: Buenos días, Jefe.

SOL: Luna! How goes my eternal war with the stars? ¿Cuidaste mi cielo por toda la noche?

LUNA: Simón, Jefe, the heavens are fine.

SOL: ¿Y tu hermana? Did you watch over her?

LUNA: Sí, señor. ¡Cómo no!

SOL: ¿Pues cómo? . . . ¡CALLATE!

TIERRA: ¿Apá?

SOL: (*Gently.*) Sí, m'ija, ¿cómo estás?

TIERRA: Bien, Papá.

SOL: And all your humanity, that plague of miserable mortals you call your children? Do they still persist in their petty greed and hatred and fear of death?

TIERRA: Sí, Tata. (*To BERNABE.*) Go.

BERNABE: ¿Señor? (*Pause.*) ¿Señor de los cielos?

SOL: ¿Quién me llama?

BERNABE: It's me, Señor. Down here.

SOL: ¿Quién eres tú?

BERNABE: Bernabé.

SOL: ¿Qué? ¡LOOK AT ME!

BERNABE: (*Shielding his eyes.*) Bernabé . . . I come to tell you
    something, Señor . . . de mi amor . . .
SOL: (*Disdainfully.*) ¿Amor?
BERNABE: Por la Tierra.
SOL: ¡¿M'ija!?
BERNABE: (*Humbly.*) Con todo respeto, señor.
SOL: (*Pause.*) Many centuries have passed, Bernabé, since men
    remembered who is el padre de la tierra. En verdad, very
    few have ever had the courage to face me, como es debido.
    Why have you come?
BERNABE: I am a man, Señor.
SOL: ¿Y eso qué me importa a mí?
BERNABE: I love her.
SOL: (*Scoffing majestically.*) Ha! Billions of men have loved
    her. Do you think you are the first? Look at her, Bernabé,
    this is la Tierra who has been all things to all men. Madre,
    prostituta, mujer. Aren't you afraid?
BERNABE: (*Bravely.*) No, Señor, of what?
SOL: ¡De su PADRE, desgraciado! ¡¡¡EL SOL!!! (*There is a
    terrifying flash of light and thunder. BERNABE runs and
    hides.*) Look at him running like a coward! ¡MALHORA!
    I should kill you for what your kind has done to m'ija!
BERNABE: It wasn't me, Señor!
TIERRA: (*Stepping forward.*) ¡Por favor, Tata! ¡Es inocente!
LUNA: Es cierto, Jefe. The vato's a Chicano. He's never had
    any tierra!
SOL: (*Pause, calms down.*) What is your work, Bernabé?
BERNABE: I work in the fields.
SOL: You are dirt poor, then?
BERNABE: Sí, Señor.
SOL: Then, how do you intend to take care of my daughter? You
    have no money! You have no POWER!
BERNABE: (*Pause.*) Señor, I am nobody, that's true. In town
    people say I'm only a loco. But I know one thing, that the
    rich people are more locos than me. They sell la Tierra all

the time, in little pedacitos here and there, but I know she should never be sold like that . . . because she doesn't belong to anyone. Like a woman should never be sold, ¿qué no? Eso es lo que pienso, Señor. If anybody has hurt la Tierra, it's not the pobres, it's the men with money and power. I can only love her.

LUNA: (*Sotto voce.*) ¡Orale, te aventates, ese! (EL SOL *silences* LUNA *with a powerful glance.*)

SOL: Dices bien. (*Pause.*) Now I know who you are, Bernabé. Eres el último y el primero . . . The last of a great noble lineage of men I once knew in ancient times, and the first of a new raza cósmica that shall inherit the earth. Your face is a cosmic memory, Bernabé. It reminds me of an entire humanity, de tus mismos ojos, tu piel, tu sangre. They too loved la Tierra and honored su padre above all else. They too were my children. They pierced the human brain and penetrated the distant stars and found the hungry fire that eats of itself. They discovered what today only a loco can understand — that life is death, and that death is life. Que la vida no vale nada porque vale todo. That you are one, so you can be two, two so you can be four, and then eight, and then sixteen, and on and on until you are millions, billions! — only to return once again to the center and discover . . . nada, so you fill up the space with one again. ¿Me comprendes, Bernabé? What power was that?

BERNABE: El poder del Sol, Señor?

SOL: (*Pauses.*) Tienes razón . . . and that's why if you unite with m'ija, you shall have that poder. And you shall be my Son! Tierra, do you love this man?

TIERRA: Sí, Papá.

SOL: Bernabé, ¿de veras quieres a la Tierra?

BERNABE: Con todo el corazón.

SOL: (*Ironically.*) ¿Corazón? No, hijo, not with your corazón. You may love her with your body, your blood, your seed, but your heart belongs to me. ¿Estás listo para morir?

BERNABE: ¡Morir!

SOL: ¡Para vivir! (BERNABE *is momentarily stunned and confused. He looks at* LA LUNA *and* LA TIERRA. *They say nothing.*)

BERNABE: Señor, I don't want to die.

SOL: Hijo, I offer you the power of the Sun. You have been nothing, now you shall be everything. Yo soy el comienzo y el fin de todas las cosas. Believe in me and you shall never die. Will you give me your corazón?

BERNABE: (*Pause.*) Sí, Señor.

SOL: ¡Que sea así! (*Drums and flutes.* BERNABE *is sacrificed.* LA TIERRA *and* LA LUNA *lay his body out.*)

SOL: ¡Bernabé, levántate! (BERNABE *rises — a complete man.*) For here on you shall be un hombre nuevo and you shall help me to conquer the stars! (BERNABE *walks erect.*) Bernabé, la Tierra es virgen y tuya. Sean felices.

TIERRA: ¡Bernabé! (BERNABE *and* LA TIERRA *embrace.*)

LUNA: ¡Orale! Congratulations, loco — I mean, ese. ¡A toda madre!

SOL: ¡SILENCIO PUES! (*Pause.*) The day is dying. The hour has come for me to go. Mis hijos, I leave you with my blessings. (*Blesses them.*) Luna, stand vigil over my cielo through the darkest night, and give light to your hermana, eh?

LUNA: Sí, Jefe, like always.

SOL: Bueno, me voy pues. Bernabé, Tierra, tengan hijos . . . muchos hijos. (*Starts to sink.*)

TIERRA: Buenas noches, Papá.

LUNA: Buenas noches, Jefe.

BERNABE: Buenas noches, Señor.

SOL: (*Sinking fast.*) Buenas noches . . . Bernabé! (SOL *is gone. There is a silence.* LA TIERRA *shivers, then* BERNABE *and* LA LUNA.)

TIERRA: It's cold.

LUNA: Simón, the Jefito's gone. (*Looks up at the sky.*) Well, I better get up to my chante también. Orale, novios — what kind of moonlight would you like? Something muy romantic y de aquellas?

TIERRA: Never mind. Just leave.

LUNA: Mírala, mírala — just because you got married again! For the zillionth time.

BERNABE: (*With a powerful calm.*) Mira, hermano, the time for insults is over. If once I was a loco, now I am a man — and I belong to la Tierra, as she belongs to me. So, good night.

LUNA: Okay, 'ta bien, pues. I gotta get to work anyway. (*Looks up.*) Fat-assed stars! I bet you they're just itching to horn in on Jefe's territory. I better go keep 'em in line. Buenas noches, pues, y don't be afraid to get down and dirty, eh? ¡Orale! (*LA LUNA exits. LA TIERRA turns her back on BERNABE.*)

TIERRA: ¿Bernabé?

BERNABE: ¿Qué?

TIERRA: Will you love me — ¿para siempre?

BERNABE: Siempre.

TIERRA: ¡Hasta la muerte? (*She turns. Her face is a death mask.*)

BERNABE: Hasta la muerte. (*They embrace.*)

SEVEN

BERNABE'*s house. EL TIO comes in quickly, looking over his shoulder. MADRE is at the door of her house.*

MADRE: Teodoro, ¿qué paso? Did you find m'ijo?

TIO: What are you doing in the street, hermanita? Get into the house, ándale!

MADRE: ¿Pa' qué? To worry even more?

TIO: ¡El sol está muy caliente!

MADRE: I don't care if it's hot! What happen with m'ijo?

(*Pause.*) ¿Qué pasó, pues, hombre? Did they find him? Miserable wino, what good are you? Bernabé's your nephew, but nothing worries you, verdad? Did I tell you to go look in the pozo he made? (*Pause.*) You went, verdad? You know something! ¿Qué pasó, hombre? (*She looks down the street.*) Ay, Teodoro, some men are coming. Eduardo is with them! They're bringing a body. ¡Válgame Dios! (MADRE *starts to run forward.* TIO *stops her.*)

TIO: Stay here, hermanita!

MADRE: (*Starting to get hysterical.*) NO, ¡déjame ir! ¡Déjame ir! It's m'ijo. You know it is, ¿verdad? ¿Qué pasó? ¿Qué pasó?

TIO: Está muerto.

MADRE: ¡Ay! (*Gasps. Can't get breath.*)

TIO: We found him—buried in the earth. (TORRES *and* PRIMO *bring in* BERNABE's *body. They lay him down, covered with a canvas. Now* MADRE *releases a long, sorrowful cry as she leans over the body.*)

MADRE: M'ijo! M'IJITO!

PRIMO: It's all my fault, tío. Fue toda mi culpa.

TIO: No, hijo, don't blame yourself. You only wanted to help him. This was God's will. Fue por la voluntad de Dios. (*Drums and flutes. In the sky above and behind them,* BERNABE *and* LA TIERRA *appear in a cosmic embrace. He is naked, wearing only a loincloth. She is Coatlicue, Mother Earth, the Aztec Goddess of Life, Death, and Rebirth.*)

Pensamiento Serpentino

A Chicano Approach to the
Theatre of Reality

Luis Valdez

"Cada cabeza es un mundo"

Teatro

eres el mundo
y las paredes de los
buildings más grandes
son

nothing but scenery.

The dialogue
de esta gran pantomima
de la tierra
is written in English
en German
en Francaise
in Spanish
in Italiano
en Tagalog

It is a giant improvisation
con role-playing
by men and women
y las razas del mundo
playing master and slave
rich and poor

black and white

pero underneath it all
is the truth
the Spiritual Truth
that determines all materia

la energía that creates the

universe
la fuerza con purpose
la primera cause de todo
even before the huelga
la First Cause de Creation

Dios

El Director de la Great Force
o Gran Tragedia
depending on your predelection

Los indios knew of this
long ago
hace muchos años que cantaban
en su flor y canto
de las verdades
CIENTIFICAS Y RELIGIOSAS

del mundo

Sin embargo
However

We were conquistados
and COLONIZADOS
and we (de la raza de bronce)
began to think we were EUROPEOS
and that their vision of reality
was
IT.

But REALITY es una Gran Serpiente
a great serpent
that moves and changes

and keeps crawling
out of its
dead skin

despojando su pellejo viejo
to emerge
clean and fresh
la nueva realidad nace
de la realidad vieja

And so
los oprimidos del mundo
continue to become
los liberadores

in the true progress of cosas

and the Chicano is part of the
process

el proceso cósmico that will
LIBERATE OUR CONQUISTADORES
or their descendents

así es que el gachupín y el gabacho
will be Mexicanized

but first el CHICANO must Mexicanize
himself
para no caer en cultural trampas

and that means that

not Thomas Jefferson nor Karl Marx
will LIBERATE the Chicano

not Mahatma Ghandi nor Mao Tze Tung
IF HE IS NOT LIBERATED FIRST BY
HIS PROPIO PUEBLO
BY HIS POPOL VUH
HIS CHILAM BALAM
HIS CHICHEN ITZA
KUKULCAN, GUCUMATZ, QUETZALCOATL.

Y qué lindo es estudiar
lo de su pueblo de uno

We must all become NEO-MAYAS
Porque los Mayas
really had it together

DIOS
Hunab Ku
El único dador de la medida
y EL MOVIMIENTO
was a mathematically moral
concept of the supreme being
EL SEÑOR DE LOS ASTROS.

RELIGION and SCIENCE were
una sola cosa
para los mayas de la antigüidad

just look at their moral concept
IN LAK'ECH: *Tú Eres Mi Otro Yo*

which they derived from
studying the sun spots.

Their communal life
was not based on intellectual

173

agreement
it was based on a vision
of los cosmos
porque el hombre pertenecía
a las estrellas

Así es que the Christian
concept of Love Thy Neighbor
as Thyself was engrained into
their daily behavior

they wouldn't think of
acting any other way

Because you that read this
are me
and I who write this am you
and I wish you well wherever
you are
Que Dios camine contigo.

IN LAK'ECH: Si te amo y te respeto
a ti, me amo y me respeto yo;
si te hago daño a ti, me hago daño a mí.

That, carnales, was LEY AND ORDER
whatever I do to you
I do to myself

Even the United States
of America will someday learn
that it cannot bomb Hanoi
without inflicting violence on itself

And neither can YOU

insult a brother
do violence to a sister
Hate somebody
without that ODIO
coming back to you
somewhere
sometime
en alguna forma

Porque ésa es THE LAW
the scientific and religious
LEY of the universe.

To be CHICANO is not (NOT)
to hate the gabacho or the
gachupín or even the pobre
vendido . . .

To be CHICANO is to love yourself
your culture, your
skin, your language

And once you become CHICANO
that way
you begin to love other people
otras razas del mundo
los vietnamitas
los argentinos
los colombianos
and, yes, even los europeos
because they need us more
than we need them.

But, above all
to be CHICANO is to LOVE GOD.

For I have never read a single
poem by an Azteca, Tolteca, Maya
or Yaqui ATHEIST

Todos los indios creen en Dios.

In order to fully
EVOLVE
(evolucionar con la
serpiente)
the Chicano Movement
must
MOVE
con el MOVEMENT
of the Cosmos
with the NAHUI OLLIN
el quinto sol,
SOL DE MOVIMIENTO

It must move with the
EARTH, LA TIERRA,
It must move with the
MORNING STAR, VENUS
Quetzalcóatl, Jesucristo
it must move with GOD.

RELIGION (re-ligion)
is nothing more than the
tying back
RE-LIGARE
with the cosmic center

As Chicanos
As Neo Mayas

we must re-identify
with that center and proceed
outward with love and strength
AMOR Y FUERZA
and undying dedication to justice

Justice between man and woman
Justice between man and nature
Justice between man and god.

They all happen at once.

Jesucristo is Quetzalcóatl
The colonization is over
La Virgen de Guadalupe is Tonantzín
The suffering is over
The universe is Aztlán
The revolution is now.

European concepts of reality
ya no soplan.
Reason alone no es todo el cuento
El indio baila
He DANCES his way to truth
in a way INTELLECTUALS will
never understand

El corazón
(YOLLO en nahuatl-*movimiento*)
feels a reality the mind
the human mind
cannot grasp.

EL ESPIRITU
the spirit

is stronger than
flesh and bone and stone
and death.

Y por eso al descubrir
a Quetzalcóatl
Kukulcan
Gucumatz
Chichen Itza
Mexico
(todos son la misma cosa)

we go beyond all
las formas culturales
of the human race
and discover universal
truth

Jesucristo como Dios
died for all of us
ONCE
and annihilated LA MUERTE

Dying

on the cross
Jesus Christ spoke
in a strange
and holy
language, saying:

"HELI, HELI, LAMAH ZABAC TANI"
which was misinterpreted
long ago as

"MY GOD, MY GOD, WHY HAST
THOU FORSAKEN ME?"
Because the translators
did not recognize
the strange phrase
which was

in

MAYA YUCATECO
and meant

"AHORA ME SUMERGIO EN LA
ALBORADA DE TU PRESENCIA"

which was la presencia de Dios
Who had not forsaken His Son at all.

EL ESPIRITU is greater than
all differences between
languages
peoples
races
places
times

even greater than the
difference between

life and death

The MAYAS knew this and that is
why CHRIST knew the MAYAS.

Para el hombre cósmico

EL CAN de los mayas antiguos
la muerte no existe
Racial distinctions
no existen
límites materiales
no existen
nation, wealth, fashions,
hatreds, envidias, greed
the lust for power
no existen,

not even the lust for
CHICANO POWER.

Como los curanderos
abusados
El hombre CAN (consciencia cósmica)
se vuelve pájaro
o animal o pescado
y se mete al río a descansar.

He can be everything
because he LOVES everything
(menos el diablo)

he identifies with TODO

So he IS todo

And that, carnales
is truly being

Chi-CAN-o.
Mexico, after all, means
feathered serpent

or, if you are mathematically
trucha, it means
$E=MC2$

Así va la onda:
MEEXICANOOB
is an old word
pronounced MESHICANOB
y quiere decir
SERPIENTES BARBADAS
porque la word
MEEX means barba (beard)
and combines with KIN
(sol) to give us the
concept of BARBAS DE
LOS RAYOS DEL SOL
which refers to the
golden feathers of QUETZALCOATL.

These are all MAYAN words
and have been traced in
their complex roots and
combinations by Domingo
Martínez Paredes
in his books:

Un Continente y Una Cultura,
El Popol Vuh Tiene Razón,
El Idioma Maya Hablado y Escrito

pero

MEEX-KIN-CO
(co means serpiente also)
eventually gives us

MEXICO
which means
serpiente emplumada
and according to the
mathematical interpretation
of the Mayas
refers to the
espiritual-material duality
of all things

Matter and Energy

Which in European terms
thanks to Einstein
is the theory of relativity
and his formula

$E=MC2$

And you know what?
It simply means

that LOVE is stronger than HATE

That the Universe is one big
YES!
Even for those of you that
read this and say no, chale,
nel, puro pedo.

Like it or not
cuando te mueres
no te mueres
you go to the next barrio
de tu evolución

y le sigues dando
hasta que quedas limpiecito
y lleno de good intentions
para que ya no te hagas
harm a ti mismo.

You make your own hell or heaven
como lo quieres
and if you feel oppressed
pues LIBERATE!
Because all you have to do
is start fighting for your own
liberation and you become FREE
LIBRE
como los rayos del sol.

Money, clothes, political power
will not make you free
only the STRUGGLE
LA LUCHA para ser libre y de
buen corazón will liberate you

Y cuando te sientes agüitado
and you are depressed
and feeling helpless
send out a little CARIÑO
and it will come back to you
faster than light.

You will feel its heat
CALOR, fuerza
levantándote
liberándote

And if you die

in the struggle

pos a toda madre
También
porque los
revolucionarios cósmicos
NO MUEREN

I don't mean they live
in the memory of the people
or something like that

I mean: NO MUEREN!

Se van a las estrellas
y los astros
y conviven
con Dios

para siempre

Pero mientras que estás
en este mundo
ACT

Don't pretend
ACT (ACTUA) in reality
and that means in the
greater reality beyond
the limited world or
reality of the gabacho or
European intellectual.

ACT on the stage of the universe
con DIOS en el corazón

como decían los Aztecas

Chicano time por ejemplo
has never been gabacho time
because the Chicano exists
in time with the temporadas
and the movement of the plánets
and the stars.

Once we start moving in tune
con las estrellas
the time of the wristwatch
nos cae huango.

The wristwatch is a game
an arbitrary improvisation
invented by Europe.

Measure your time against
la calaca, LA MUERTE
Si eres materialist
a solid contemplation
of DEATH will show you
that you haven't got
too much time
to waste.

Better make it count now.
PERO cuando te das cuenta
de la verdadera movida de
DIOS
Time and Death become unimportant
como todos los empty goals
de este mundo.

Porque la patada of existence is in
BEING JUST
and the best way to be
just is to treat everything
like you treat yourself
because (even if you can't
grasp it all de repente)
YOU ARE EVERYTHING.

Y así nos dijeron los MAYAS
a long time ago
por eso dejaron los pocos
libros, poemas, pinturas
que dejaron
(los gachupines quemaron lo demás)
para que nos diéramos cuenta.

Whatever you do
DO NOT GO TO THE MAYAS
TO ANY OF OUR INDIGENA FOREFATHERS
WITH ANTHROPOLOGY IN YOUR MIND

Por ahi no hay nada

Tienes que cruzar el puente
and BELIEVE.

O como decían entonces
con la palabra MEN:
(Mayan not English) Creer
para Crear para Hacer.

Sólo así se hacen las cosas:

CON CREENCIAS.

Y comienza con creencia en
EL SEÑOR
El great playwright del universe
el scene designer y costume maker

El make-up man del teatro
infinito
que nos pone el maquillaje
brown, white, black, yellow

El que no hace feos o bonitos
aunque no nos gusta

The point is to participate
in the play
not to reject the parts
we are given to play.

Es todo improvisación anyway.

Make your own play.

That's what el Gran Director
de los Astros wants you to do.
Whatever plot you can come up with

He already wrote it desde cuando.

¿Y sabes qué?
It has a lot of meaning.

A ti te dio tu papel (role)
for very special reasons.
Nobody else has your part,

or tu máscara or tus lines.

If you think you got a bit
part, pos a la mejor it's the
best part in the whole
production

Porque el Señor no hace las
cosas así nomás.

He knows what He's doing.

Tienes que love tu part
and play it like an expert.

Don't try to steal somebody
else's role
don't try to act like
somebody else tampoco
cada quien tiene su tiempo
y espacio
and nobody can play you
better than you.

If a Chicano rejects his part
and starts playing Gabacho
he's going to mess up

Tiene que comenzar con lo suyo

Once he learns how to be Chicano
and he proves himself to be
un actor a toda madre
entonces las otras parts
le comienzan a llover

He gets to play a Black
or a Chino or a Swede
Because there's nothing
El Mero Mero del Teatro
Universal likes better
than versatility, mano.

Y cuando el Chicano puede
decirle a todo el mundo:

Raza, te comprendo y te
quiero because I know
where you're coming from
and where you're going

Desde Borneo al Congo
Desde Moscow a Mercedes,
todos son mi Raza
Humana—

ENTONCES EL CHICANO SE
SALE DE SUS HUESOS,
SE SALE DE LA PINTA DE SU
CARNE

Y ya no es "minority group"
ya no es un hyphenated
Spanish-speaking person

es un HOMBRE, un SER HUMANO,
un hijo de Dios.

Y si le da la gana hace su
papel de Chicano como expert

hablando en Swahili
refinándose un plato bien
filipino de adobo

porque a los hijos de Dios
les encanta
hacer todos los papeles
del teatro del mundo
y los hacen

con huevos

Y este papel de Teatro
de esta vida
es lo que los Mayas
called tu NAC.

Tu límite.
Tu medida.
Tu forma.

Pero adentro de ese límite
está el espíritu
que no tiene límite
y por eso
the Mayans called it
CAN which is the reverse
of NAC.

Once you learn your limitations
you encounter your infinite potential
Encuentras a DIOS EN TU CORAZON.

Pero primero you have to
KNOW YOURSELF

pos luego
how could it be otherwise?

Así es que no chismees
ni te preocupes de tus vecinos
ni les busques faltas
because the faults you find in them
are not in them: ESTAN EN TI MISMO.
That is why you can see them so
clearly.

A thief can spot another thief
in a multitude.

A teenager worried about pimples
will spot another person's pimples
a mile away.

IN LAK'ECH: Tú eres mi otro yo.

Somos espejos para cada uno.
We are mirrors to each other.

Así es que no andes criticando
o maltratando a otras gentes
deal with your own límites

The way to fight racism is with
non-racism.
The way to fight violence
is with non-violence.

Pero de todos modos ACTUA
ACT, EVOLVE
HAY EVOLUTION Y RE-EVOLUTION.

Aquí estamos en el gran
anfiteatro de los
cosmos and you are meant
to be active.

César Chávez's NON-VIOLENCE
is one of the most
violent forces around
porque es positiva y porque
comienza con Dios.

Y a los que no les caiga
todo esto
pos hay 'ta
Vietnam
con todo su amor humano
precioso espíritu positivo
que no se ha dejado vencer
¿Y qué decía el Uncle Ho?

pues que a pesar de los
bombardeos
minas
biological warfare
sangre derramada en los
rice paddies de la nación

El pueblo Vietnamita todavía
abraza al pueblo norteamericano

que no culpa a los gabachos
porque solo el gobierno es culpable

El Nixon (que Dios lo perdone)

El LBJ (que Dios lo perdone)
El Kennedy (que Dios lo perdone)
no son los United States of America.

Y ésa es la verdadera victoria
de Vietnam: el no ser tragados por

EL ODIO cuando diariamente les cae
la muerte por ensima.

Esa fuerza moral la tenemos todos
gracias a la resistencia
de esos heroicos campesinos.

En cara de esto,
how can we let the enemy
robarnos of our humanity
with a little racism and police brutality

Compared to the Vietnamese,
our life in the hands of the gringo
has been
a tardeada con pura música de acordión.

Así es que hay que learn to
handle the contradictions
in reality.

Acts of Hatred
must be countered by
Acts of Love

Instead of hating (fearing)
that GABACHO CULTURE is
swallowing us alive

WE MUST SWALLOW IT

as easily as a candy coated pill
and then continue being ourselves

in English
in Spanish
in Nahuatl
in Yaqui

and gabacho racism, capitalism
and imperialism
will flow through our tripas
but they will not harm us
for they will be eliminated
from our bodies
just like
ordinary WASTE MATTER.

(Because we are universal Justice)

Así lo hizo MAO
con su Yin Yang, ¿o apoco
China no se está tragando
toda la cultura de Europa
en un bocadito que apenas
basta para un muela?
Simón que yes.

Y si los Chinos tienen su
sabiduría antigua
pos aqui en CEM-ANAHUAC
también tenemos lo mero principal

EL NAHUI-OLLIN es el YIN YANG
como es el alfa y omega de Cristo.
Por eso vamos a vencer

porque nuestros abuelos inditos
fueron HEAVIES
y se dieron cuenta
de la medida y el movimiento
del universo.

Y FUERON HUMILDES

no egoístas
no materialistas
no cínicos

Supieron AMAR A LA OBRA DE DIOS.
And that is why Quetzalcóatl
en su leyenda
put a stop to human sacrifice
Porque el Señor no aguanta la
destrucción insensata
de su Creación.

En la América Indígena
no había MACHOS
in the Spanish sense of the word.

Había hombres bien hechos
como había Mujeres bien hechas
y los dos formaban un
natural balance

EL MACHO INDIGENA was not a KILLER OF MEN
ni wife beater

Era un hombre sabio que amaba a

los niños
los animales
las flores
los cantos

because in these living things
como en todo el mundo vivo

he saw el Plan Divino del Señor.

La visión de Quetzalcóatl
era como la visión de Jesucristo.

Cuando los indígenas dejaron
de creer en Quetzalcóatl
and they began to believe in
the Jaguar y las fuerzas de
la noche

entonces comenzo
la conquista de Mexico

y eso fue centenares de años antes
de la llegada de Hernán Cortés.

Entró Tezcatlipoca el joven
(otra forma del diablo)
y la America Indígena
caminó inevitablemente hacia
la destrucción de su civilización.

Pero no fue destrucción completa,

porque aquí estamos nosotros
todos brown y
hablando de Aztlán

Pero hay que tener cuidado
con ese diablo-Tezcatlipoca

(que es el "god of knowledge" —
worldly knowledge como lo es
Satanás with the tree of knowledge
in the Garden of Eden)

porque nos hace creer que
ya lo sabemos todo
y que GOD IS DEAD
y todo ese pedo

Y no es cierto

EL UNIVERSO
is an awe-inspiring place
y es nuestro verdadero chante.

Vamos a volar a las estrellas
sin spaceship.

Solamente hay que empezar

a vivir sin miedo

sin miedo del gabacho
sin miedo de los pigs
sin miedo del diablo

Hay que tener confianza

En la Gran Evolución de las Cosas.

TODO VA BIEN

DIOS APOYA EL DESARROLLO DEL
CHICANO SI EL CHICANO APOYA
A DIOS.

Y no hay que olvidar
que según la profecía
de los tiempos antiguos
QUETZALCOATL está por volver
al mundo.

(Tezcatlipoca su cuate malicioso
llegó en forma de Cortés la
última vez en 1519)

Pero por ahi viene el
día del nacimiento
de la SERPIENTE EMPLUMADA
(según la cuenta antigua) en
el AÑO CE ACATL EN EL DIA
CE ACATL

Y cae el 16 de agosto de 1987.

La profecía says that the
entire world will be
enlightened

and so it is.

LA CONQUISTA está por acabarse
and the Chicano is part of

that Great Spiritual ReBirth.

Men will go to the Stars
Only con Dios en su Corazón.

Así lo dispone la Evolucion
Así lo dispone THE GREAT
FEATHERED SERPENT OF THE
UNIVERSE.

Así los dispone DIOS.

Así sea.